REFLECTIONS

of my

JOURNEY

REFLECTIONS
of my
JOURNEY

A Compilation of
200 RHYTHMIC POEMS
That Will Inspire, Encourage, and Enlighten

Shirley Flowe Furr

XULON PRESS

Xulon Press
2301 Lucien Way #415
Maitland, FL 32751
407.339.4217
www.xulonpress.com

Paperback ISBN-13: 978-1-6628-2967-3
eBook ISBN-13: 978-1-6628-2968-0

DEDICATION

Most books are dedicated to a person in the author's life who has influenced them or helped them in some way. At times, the honor is given to someone they love. For all these reasons, this, my first published work, is dedicated to the third person of the Trinity, the sweet Holy Spirit of God. He has been my indweller, my friend, enabler, and teacher since I chose to follow Christ as a child. He has been my guide, my source of joy, my comforter when days were hard. It was by His promptings this book was written. It was He, who gave me the dream of writing a poetry book, as well as the mind to imagine and bring rhyme, rhythm and life to its pages. How could I take credit for these works or not give credit to the one who gave the inspiration for every line and stanza and awakened in me that dormant dream?

TABLE OF CONTENTS

Good for the Spirit

Good for the Soul

Preface

I t's said that "God is in the details." I have found this to be true. He has a good plan for every life and has gifted each individual with talents and abilities to do good things He has included in that plan. Little did I know, sixteen years before this book would be published, I was already putting my heart on paper in the form of many of the poems included here, poems that were to be part of my story.

During a very challenging time of my life, (2005-2009) I found myself writing poetry that God continuously was pouring into my spirit. During those difficult years, I wrote approximately 175 poems. At that time, I felt one day I would publish them, because God never gives us any kind of gift that he doesn't expect us to share. It was not an urgent thing. It was a dream, but a dormant one.

Things suddenly changed in February 2021 as I was reading an old devotional book entitled *Heart Talks* by C. W. Naylor. The front of the book contained a picture of the author in bed and the writing above told how he had been an invalid for thirteen years. It went on to say that he believed his condition was God's way of developing his heart and making him more useful in helping others. Having written articles and several books, he said of himself that he had been "qualified for his task by **training of the soul** in the school of suffering." Right away, God spoke to my heart, and those words "training of the soul" stood out to me. I could identify with them due to the physical and emotional pain of breast cancer, the sting of a heart-rending relationship, and the shock that after 21 years, my position was being eliminated due to a bank merger. Immediately, I wrote the poem contained in this book called **"The Training of the Soul".** I believe it to be one of the most beautiful poems God ever gave me!

Within a week I had written twenty more, and the next two months, over one hundred more. Pen and paper were always close by as I was writing daily. Some poems came to me as quickly as I could write and were scribbled on paper towels or church bulletins. Others I labored over. There was an urgency, a nudge that the Lord was saying, "Now is the time!" Another season of *my journey* was beginning. To put my poetry in book form was something I felt compelled to do and here, in your hands is the result of God bringing my hibernating dream to life!

It is my prayer, just as it was C.W. Naylor's, (whom God used to inspire my soul to take on the writing of this book) that as the reader, you will be helped somehow, whether by receiving encouragement, comfort or just a ray of hope.

May you be blessed to better understand the love of God and your relationship with Him through the thoughts in this collection of my first published work. Glory to God for allowing me to be a vessel as **"Clay in the Hands of the Potter."**

- Shirley Flowe Furr

Baby Jesus

Christ was born on
Christmas day,
Baby Jesus there He lay.
Darling baby here He stay
Pillowed soft upon the hay
Baby Jesus born today.
When He was little He
would play.
Now He is strong and knows
His way,
And can say to the
children,
Praise that wonderful
day.

By -
Shirley Flowe

BABY JESUS

Christ was born
On Christmas Day
Baby Jesus there He lay
Darling baby here He stay
Pillowed soft upon the hay
Baby Jesus born today
When He was little
He would play
Now He is strong
And knows His way
And can say to the children
Praise that wonderful day

AUTHOR'S NOTE

This poem was written when I was in the second grade at A.T. Allen Elementary School. The students in my class were given the assignment of writing a poem that would be judged by our teacher, Mrs. McManus. The best entry was to be posted in the classroom. This is an image of the paper she rewrote my poem on so it could be better seen hanging on our wall. I was excited and so proud to have won, but now realize even at that young age, God had planted in me the seed of poetry. He's good to bring about His purposes in our lives that way!

A True Dream

If you have a dream, just go for it -
You'll never know till you try;
Don't let questions and hesitations stop you,
Make your dream a reality before you die.

It may have been for years and long hours,
The idea has floated around in your head;
Don't let fear of failure or criticism stop you,
Don't let apprehension fill you with dread.

Don't listen to others who plant their doubts,
If it's a *true dream* God put in your heart;
Don't tell yourself you can't do it -
Cause you can, and He'll do His part.

You might've just been given an amazing idea,
Or it could be a farfetched, way out plan;
Whether it's in development or it's just cropped up,
A *true dream* will become a demand.

Perhaps for a while this dream has been dormant,
But in your heart God has kept it alive;
You can never deny it or get away from it,
Is your inner man telling you "It's time"?

AUTHOR'S NOTE

The first poem written after signing with Xulon Press, my publisher. God inspired this one as soon as I finished my consultation. My dream was becoming a reality and so can yours!

POETRY IN MY SPIRIT

Lord, I'm so excited
You've lit a fire under me;
You've put *poetry in my spirit*
That you want many eyes to see.

Lord, lead me through this process
It's something I know nothing about;
You've given me words to put on paper
Now, help me get my poetry out.

When my book is finally completed
The labor and the work is all done;
I'll look back with a sigh and lift my hands high
Giving glory to your precious Son.

SCRIPTURE REFERENCES
Philippians 2:13 ~ Ecclesiastes 3:1-8

AUTHOR'S NOTE

The 2nd poem written, (1st poem was "A True Dream") after signing with Xulon Press to create my dream of a book of poetry.

Good for the Spirit

GOOD FOR THE SPIRIT

The life of every human consists of body, *spirit*, and soul. This section contains poems that relate to the *spirit*. Of the three parts of man, the *spirit* is the innermost part of our being and is the most noble. It is our God consciousness and the place of His dwelling with man. No other creature has this element of humanity which gives us the privilege of connecting and communicating with the Holy, Almighty God. We worship, fellowship, serve, have faith in, and pray to God who is Spirit through our *spirit*.

Just as a radio (after being given power), receives invisible radio waves through which to create sounds of music and words, so the *spirit of man* contacts and receives the Spirit of God and is then given the means for Godly expression. So, when the word *spirit* is used, it is in reference to the part of mankind which communes with God. The more we through our *spirit* seek and fellowship with the Spirit of God, the more our souls will acknowledge His part and His place in our lives.

SCRIPTURE REFERENCES
Proverbs 20:27 ~ Ecclesiastes 12:7 ~ Luke 1:46-47, 23:46 ~ John 3:6, 4:24
Romans 1:9, 8:10, 16 ~ I Corinthians 2:14 ~ Ephesians 1:17
I Thessalonians 5:23

ANGELS

It was an *angel* who announced the birth of Jesus,
To the shepherds, brought glad tidings.
Angels ministered strength in Gethsemane,
When Satan His mind tried dividing.

To do the will of the Father,
He was sent to Earth for thirty-three years.
As He ministered, taught and labored,
Angels walked with Him wiping His tears.

He died on the cross and was buried,
In a borrowed tomb He was laid.
Angels rolled the great stone away,
In the presence of soldiers so afraid.

The Bible tells us to be careful,
We may entertain *angels* unaware.
So just open your eyes and you'll see them,
God has placed them everywhere.

Earth's human *angels* minister to us,
Different forms you'll find they take.
A neighbor, a preacher, a carpenter,
Of anyone an Earth *angel* He can make.

All it takes is a heart to serve Him,
Meeting needs along the way.
Not doing good deeds to get noticed,
Or rewarded on judgment day.

Only because He loves us,
And pass it on we should,
Cause we'll never make it to Heaven,
Just by doing or being good.

Get behind me Satan,
Angels back me up to say.
When He would try to steal my joy,
And on my mind would prey.

When I draw my last breath on Earth,
A heavenly host will escort me away.
To the presence of My Father,
I'll meet Jesus, My Savior that day.

In formation as *angels* stand at attention,
I'll walk through a line of drawn swords.
Representing the Holy Bible,
God's precious, infallible Word,

The *angels* will stand in wonder,
To participate they'll know not how.
As saved ones sing "Amazing Grace",
And our knees to the King we bow.

Angels' swords held high in honor
Represent truths lived by, died by, believed.
Those swords held high in honor too,
Of the one who died for me.

SCRIPTURE REFERENCES
Luke 2:8-14, 16:22, 22:43 ~ Ephesians 2:8-9 ~ I Peter 1:12

BE A WINNER

You can always *be a winner,*
Put your life in Jesus' hands;
Doesn't meant all things will be perfect,
But when you can't stand, He can.

Stay in the fight, do what's right,
For that, you will one day be glad;
Everybody won't like it, but that's ok,
You'll be stronger through experiences had.

No you surely won't win all life's battles,
But in His hands you're always secure;
Just keep pushing along, let Him fight for you,
His victory is already yours.

Don't take matters into your own hands,
Don't open every available door;
Let Him direct your path and guide,
To desired places you've never seen before.

In disease, disaster, devastation,
Through hard nights and long days of pain;
During death, depression, and darkness,
Your strength He will faithfully sustain.

Yes, even when the toughest of things overtake,
Your body and your tired, weary mind;
You'll find in God a refuge,
When your spirit and His will, entwine.

SCRIPTURE REFERENCES
Deuteronomy 33:37 ~ II Chronicles 20:15 ~ Nehemiah 8:10 ~ Psalm 46:1,
73:26 ~ Proverbs 3:5-6 ~ Isaiah 58:11 ~ Hosea 14: 9 ~ Ephesians 6:12

BE STILL

Living life in a such a hurried pace
Living life in the human rat race
Never having time to seek God's face
Never fully acknowledging His amazing grace...
Whoa, slow it all down, give me a nod
Realize I'm the creator and by sin you're flawed
Realize I'm the source of all you've got
Realize I am all that you are not...
It hurts to see you going nonstop
Don't let Satan or your busy-ness
Of you godliness rob.

SCRIPTURE REFERENCES
Psalm 46:10

BETTER, GREATER, MORE

First thing, look outside, sun is shining,
Got to get on down the road.
But before I do let me honor you,
My day should be yours I know.

I'll seek your face this morning,
Asking what would you have me do.
THIS IS THE DAY THE LORD HAS MADE,
I will rejoice and use it for you.

I trust that you will guide me,
Never traveled today's *journey* before.
My attitude is to be your servant,
Living in the joy of my Lord.

To guide me, guard me, go with me,
These promises you have made.
Father, I seek to exalt your name,
And your will to obediently obey.

This day is open wide with opportunity,
It's filled with potential galore.
So today, my heart's strongest desire,
Is to *know you better, serve you greater, love you more.*

SCRIPTURE REFERENCES
Deuteronomy 11:15 ~ Psalm 118:24 ~ John 12:26 ~ II Peter 3:18

AUTHOR'S NOTE

Years ago as I was praying I told God "I want to know you better, love you greater, and serve you more." As soon as I said those words, I was alerted in my spirit as to how beautiful and meaningful they were. This is still my prayer as I daily journey on this adventure called life.

By Faith

We walk *by faith*
Not by sight
By His power
Not human might
The things unseen
The things unknown
Through faith in Him
Those things are shown

NO FAITH - Mark 13:58
LITTLE FAITH - Matthew 14:31
GREAT FAITH - Matthew 15:28

Of no faith, little faith, great faith...
Which of these describes you?
If only faith you have
As a mustard seed,
Your mountains God will move.

SCRIPTURE REFERENCES
II Corinthians 5:7 ~ Ephesians 2:8

Carry Me

It's when I'm weak that you *carry me,*
It's when my way is not known;
It's when I've stumbled and felt the hurt,
It's when my strength is all gone.

It's when my heart is weary,
It's when I seemingly can't go on;
It's then you lift me close to your heart,
And I know I'm not alone.

It's in days of clouds and thunder,
It's in the darkness of the storm;
It's in you, I've found a refuge,
It's in you, I'm safe from harm.

It's in times of casting cares,
It's in days of trial and testing;
It's in peacefulness and quiet confidence,
It's in your everlasting arms I'm found resting.

When my way is dark and dreary,
You cause me to clearly see;
When I can't find the will to walk,
It's then that you *carry me!*

SCRIPTURE REFERENCES
Isaiah 46:4 ~ Psalm 28:8-9

———— ✺ ————

AUTHOR'S NOTE

Written 4 days prior to breast cancer surgery.

Cast Your Cares

Why worry about the future?
Why worry about the past?
The things that keep us unsettled
Are things that don't usually last.

Cast your cares upon Jesus;
His shoulders can bear the load..
After all, you weren't meant to carry
Those burdens on down life's road.

Go ahead, give it up, turn it over;
Mentally release it to the Master.
He'll carry you and your worries;
You're sure to feel better much faster.

SCRIPTURE REFERENCES
Psalm 55:22, 68:19-20 ~ I Peter 5:7

Choose Triumph

Don't let yourself be defeated
Choose to live triumphantly!
Jesus already won the battle
So act like you know victory!

SCRIPTURE REFERENCES
Deuteronomy 20:4 ~ I Samuel 17:47 ~ I John 5:4

When this poem was written, a lot was going on in my life. The combination of those things had taken a toll on my physical, emotional, and spiritual well-being. God gave me triumph over the enemies of my spirit and soul BUT when this poem was penned, that victory was not yet a reality in my life. It was, however, a reality as I looked through eyes of faith!

———— ⧼⧽ ————

CLAY IN THE HANDS OF THE POTTER

Arise and go to the potter's house,
And I will cause you to hear...
So, I went down to the potter's house,
And a work He wrought on the wheel.

A vessel of clay He managed,
But marred in His hands it became;
He molded and shaped it over anew,
It was good but clay, still the same.

Then the Word of the Lord came saying:
"Oh child cannot I do with you,
As *clay in the hands of the potter,*
Your future is what I have in view.

A vessel of honor I'm shaping,
Tho' marred and broken you may feel;
I have in mind good things for you,
And my love for you is so real.

As *clay in the hands of the potter,*
The changes you feel may hurt;
But clay without the potter,
Is just a mound of dirt.

My goal is for you to be useful,
My purposes to fulfill;
To live a life of lasting value,
As the clay of your life bows its will."

SCRIPTURE REFERENCES
Jeremiah 18:1-6

DARK NIGHT OF THE SOUL

Sometimes great challenges await us,
As we face the *dark night of the soul;*
Sometimes fears can possess us,
As we face troubles we cannot control.

Through these times God works within us,
He seeks to bring us up higher;
Although it may seem He's hiding his face,
As we go through the fire.

His desire for us is to *rise up,*
To bring us to a new level;
Satan's desire is that we *give up,*
So stand up, don't give in to the devil!

The Lord's fierce passion for His children,
Compels His loving correction at times;

His affections for us, like a fire that consumes,
Burning up all debris in our lives.

He seeks in His wisdom to teach us,
Truths we'd learn by no other means;
To *humble* us, *alert* us or *awaken* us,
He never leaves us tho' sometimes it seems.

He's taking us to places we've not ventured,
Leading us thru pathways unknown;
Training us to become more lovesick,
As we realize what great love He's shown.

Causing us to fervently pursue Him,
With a heart that will faithfully obey;
Removing fear, doubt, and all obstruction,
That would block or stand in growth's way.

Hunger for God born of desperation,
A longing from which deep pain stems;
Weaning us from the ways of this world,
Creating a strong addiction to Him.

This *dark night of the soul* you face,
Is initiated by a loving Father;
Don't think it's new, you're not alone,
It's known by many others!

No child, this thing that's taken charge,
This thing you're "going thru";
Is a road that's traveled frequently,
By all whom God has used.

We struggle as we ask ourselves,
Just how long is the "dark night"?
Then we read, "JOY COMES IN THE MORNING",

And we know it'll soon be alright!

Yes, it's true, God has proven it time and again -
Joy does come in the morn;
But not before the soul emerges,
Battle scarred, more mature and war torn.

SCRIPTURE REFERENCES
Psalm 30:1-5, 34:4, 42:1~ Hebrews 12:6 ~ I Peter 5:8

DECISIONS

Decisions we all make 'em...
Then they turn around and make us.
What does your mind tell you?
Well, the mind you can't always trust.

Many *decisions* are "quite simple",
Why waste time on them, some say?..."
But yesterday's *decisions*,
Made you who you are today.

Some things require very little thought,
Some things require that we ponder...
When seeing the results of some actions,
"Did they think about that?" we may wonder.

Some *decisions* we just breeze through,
Others are simply life changing...
Sometimes those are the ones we'd like to take back,
When the future requires rearranging.

Think for yourself...
Use your own head.
Don't let others' poor choices
Cause you to feel dread.

Yes, they truly do make us or break us...
Wrong decisions lead to wrong endings.
Know that Jesus can help you decide,
In Him, you can have new beginnings.

To make Jesus your Lord and Savior,
There is no more serious choice...
When the roll is called in Heaven one day,
At your name's call in that *decision*, you'll rejoice!

SCRIPTURE REFERENCES
Proverbs 13:20 ~ Acts 16:30-31 ~ Romans 10:9-10 ~ II Timothy 1:9

DON'T GIVE UP

Hang tight! Hold on to your convictions!
Don't listen to all that's said!
If you constantly tend to dwell on it,
You'll give up due to fear and regret.

By yourself you cannot make it,
Don't feel like you're so alone;
When it seems friends and family have vanished,
When it seems all hope is gone.

There is a friend who sticks closer,
Than even a sister or a brother;

A friend who'll be there till the end,
A friend much unlike any other.

There may be times when you're just existing,
Life may need a reality check;
Times when you feel that your entire world
Is headed for a terrible train wreck.

If that's the case and you feel like
You're no doubt in for a collision;
Let me provide some wisdom today
To help you make the best decision.

When the weight of the world looms heavy,
Like an anchor that's been tied to your neck;
Look up, call His name and you'll sense Him there,
He'll keep your perspective in check.

Don't give up!! Keep going! You can do it!
You'd be surprised how much you can bear;
God will send comfort through the Spirit, your helper,
There's no other who cares like He cares.

SCRIPTURE REFERENCES
Proverbs 18:24 ~ Isaiah 54:10 ~ Zephaniah 3:17 ~ II Timothy 4:7
Hebrews 13:5

DON'T WORRY ABOUT TOMORROW

If you want to find great beauty,
Just look to the fowls of the air.
If you want to find great comfort,
Just think of how they have no cares.

The Heavenly Father feeds them;
They have no need to sow or reap.
He watches over everyone;
Their lives He lovingly keeps.

They gather at my feeders daily;
I watch as they perch upon a limb.
They're not even worried, not the least bit stressed;
Why? It's because they depend on Him.

He tells us to observe the little birds,
The tiniest sparrow, He sees fall.
If He can take care of these lowly creatures,
Then, He'll surely take care of us all.

So, friends, *don't worry about tomorrow,*
What you'll have to wear, eat or drink,
To Him, you are much more valuable than they;
He can supply all your needs, dont'cha think?

SCRIPTURE REFERENCES
Matthew 6:26

DYING DAY

When people gather 'round me on my *dying day,*
I'd like to know the kind of things that they will have to say.

Will they speak about my giving of the small wealth I've amassed?
Will they talk about the good deeds I did before I passed?

Will they tell about the heartaches and troubles I've been through?
Will they say you should'a known her, she'd have been a friend to you?

Oh all these I sure hope so. I think they'd make the list
Of things others will talk about on my final day of this.

Will they talk about my laughter? Hear it ring from day to day?
As they go about their business will they remember how I'd pray?

For those who had a problem, for those in trouble or pain,
For those whose days were burdened with less sunshine and more rain?

Will they speak of how I faltered, made mistakes along the way,
Of how they picked me up, and encouraged my soul toward a better day?

Of how I thought I knew it all, sometimes dominating our conversation,
Telling them "I told you so" while feeling great satisfaction?

Will they speak the truth about my life and share my imperfections?
Will they speak of my reputation and how I gave it protection?

Will they long once more to be with me and share friendship in some way?
When people gather 'round me on my *dying day?*

Will they think back on the good times when we laughed, we cried, we shared?
Will they think back on the foolish things we tried when we were dared?

Will they recall the excitement, the laughter, and the tears?
Will they look back and reminisce at the fun we had through the years?

Oh, many things they'll talk about, whatever comes to mind.
I hope they say, "We loved her. You know she was our kind."

I hope they say, "When you saw her, she was always the same."
Then I hope the conversation turns to another name.

The lovely name of Jesus, the one who saved my soul.
The one who sacrificed His life. The one who made me whole.

It was He who gave me the laughter. It was He who dried the tears.
It was He who gave me the wisdom and strength to live out all my years.

Yes, the lovely name of Jesus is the one I want to extol.
His is the name I want remembered. He deserves glory for it all.

It's through His power, His grace, and His love I walked on earth those days
And it's HIS precious presence that I want forever praised.

He is the reason for everything. He gave us life, you know.
Not for our honor, glory, or praise, but for His own to show.

So, if you stop in to see me on my *dying day,*
Remember this, it's not too late for you to kneel and pray.

Bring all your cares to Jesus. He knows your every need.
Bring all your sins to Jesus. He knows your every deed.

The things you feel so bad about, He died to save you from.
Through amazing grace and His sinless blood, the victory has been won.

There's nothing in the human frame–no goodness, no perfection -
That brings us to the point, of achieving God's acceptance.

The righteousness that we'd call our own, the righteousness that we'd claim,
Comes only through the cleansing power derived from Jesus' name.

So if you talk about me on my *dying day,*
Remember Jesus is the reason for any good thing you could say.

The errors and the downfalls, I'll take all the blame for them.
Just don't criticize my Savior....You'll find no fault in Him.

He's the one for whom I've lived. I'm just one for whom He died.
If you've neglected to make Him Lord, put away your foolish pride.

Make plans to meet your Maker, so you can tell friends you're "OK",
When they ask you if you're ready when it comes to your *dying day!*"

SCRIPTURE REFERENCES
John 19:30 ~ Matthew 6:8 ~ Hebrews 4:13 ~ Romans 5:9 ~ John 18:28-38
John 19:4

―――――― ∞ ――――――

AUTHOR'S NOTE

Inspired to write this poem by learning today (12/21/05) that I have breast cancer. Trusting God for healing. Not dwelling on death but caused to think more deeply about its reality.

Everything I Need

I look up to the Heavens,
From you God, comes my help.
I need your power and your wisdom,
To complete the mission I've been dealt.

This thing you've planted in my spirit,
It's a living, growing seed.
All I can say is, "Help me, Lord!"
You have *everything I need*.

SCRIPTURE REFERENCES
Psalm 121:1 ~ Ephesians 3:20 ~ Philippians 4:19

Fearfully and Wonderfully Made

Long before forming each **finger** and tiny little **toe,**
God, you knew each circumstance through which **my body** would go.

You knew the times my **heart** would beat.
You knew each word my **mouth** would speak.

You knew each breath my **lungs** would take.
You knew each print my **feet** would make.

You formed my **tongue's** sandpapery surface,
With its **taste buds** so bumpy for a wonderful purpose.

Glands, tissues, muscles, lymph nodes and cells -
Each one has its own story to tell.

For keeping up with the body's time,
You formed **membranes, vitamins, and special enzymes.**

Insulin manufacturer, **pancreas gland** with important function,
Its secretion aids digestion which gives my body unction.

Great beauty and wonders my **eyes** behold.
My roadmap of **nerves** allow me to feel hot and cold.

God, you typed the **blood** rushing through my veins.
You gave strength to the **bones** that make up my frame.

What a workhorse in my **chest**, this organ called my **heart,**
In unmatched wisdom you lovingly, created **all my parts.**

The **stomach** that assists in digesting my foods,
The **hormones** that produce the good and bad moods!

The **adrenaline** that causes me in fear to become bold.
The **temper** that causes my mama to scold.

Chemical processing tissue, my highly efficient **liver,**
Without it, no digestion, "Oh my, what a giver!"

The **ears** that keep me from being run over,
That hear loud sounds or a bee in the clover.

Body fluid passing through **kidneys and bladder,**
What a marvelous processing plant, what an intriguing matter!

The **throat** that takes in my drink like a funnel,
The **intestines** moving waste products through their dark tunnel.

The computer enclosed within my thick **skull,**
Word processor called the **brain;**
Helps me to analyze, understand and imagine,
Tells me when to get out of the rain.

The sensitive projection between mouth and eyes,
That funny looking thing called a **nose**;
With it, I smell all kinds of things,
Through it, my life's **breath** comes and goes.

The **legs** that run in a marathon race,
Or walk with a friend at a steady pace.

The **lips** that keep my mouth closed tight,
Or enjoy a sweet kiss on a moonlit night.

Teeth enameled so rock hard, allowing me to chew and bite,
Brushing twice a day keeps them pearly white.

The **hair** that protects and beautifies,
The **skin** that houses **blood and nerve** supplies.

Working as a thermostat my body temps to control,
When I'm active and overheated, the perspiration rolls!

The **organs** that provide procreation and pleasure,
God's gift to those in love–"What a beautiful treasure!"

It's true, I'm *wonderfully and fearfully made,*
For all this, you deserve full credit.
I can see perfection in your great plan,
If I'd never even read it.

Yes, my **body** is so *fearfully and wonderfully made!*
What a responsibility God has given, good health to maintain.

So Lord, let me use this vessel of clay,
Give me a desire to seek you each day.

To live out my life in light of your purpose,
To live out my life in your honorable service.

SCRIPTURE REFERENCES
Psalm 139:13-14

FOR HOW LONG

"*For how long* will this last?" you ask.
"Well, you know the future's not mine to see;
How long good or bad, be it happy or sad,
It'll last as long as it'll be.

All I know is I trust in His steadfast love,
No matter what the rolling tide brings;
Either way I'll allow my heart to rejoice,
Because my Lord has dealt bountifully with me."

SCRIPTURE REFERENCES
Psalm 13

"FREE"

The days are spent, my race is run.
My life on Earth is said and done.

No more heartaches, no more pain,
No more tears, only gain.
Safely carried to God's throne;
Safely escorted to my new home.
Friends and family have said their goodbyes.
Oh, if they could only realize
The beauty that my eyes behold;
Gates of pearl, streets of gold,
Jasper walls, many sights untold.
Others who have come before,
Greet me with love and so much more.
They say, "You're going to love this place!"
I say, I want to see His face;
The face of Him who died for me,
Who died to set my spirit *free.*
I'm *free* from everlasting death,
Free to worship, *free* to rest.
I'm *free* at last to enter in,
Free from danger, *free* from sin.
I'm *free* from worry, *free* from strife,
Free to live an everlasting life.
No more sorrows, no more loss,
All because of His death on the cross.
Home at last, I'm *free* indeed,
The creation God intended me to be.

SCRIPTURE REFERENCES
Luke 16:22 ~ I Corinthians 9:24 ~ Revelation 21:4, 21

AUTHOR'S NOTE

A tribute to the memory of my mother-in-law, **Grace Barbee Furr Allred** *written 3 days after her passing.*

From Room A7 to a Home In Heaven

My "Daddy" found his home at a living center,
For the last eight months of his life.
His final days were good ones,
No heartache, worry or strife.

He made a lot of friends there,
Played bingo, took trips, liked ring toss.
On a beautiful day in April,
Heaven's gain was our family's loss.

He was a kind hearted, gentle man,
Who tried to assist wherever he could.
If you ever needed him to help,
You knew that he surely would.

He loved to sit in the lobby,
Sharing time by the fireplace with friends.
None of us knew on that Tuesday evening,
That his life on Earth would end.

Our Heavenly Father called him home,
To a mansion in the sky.
From Room A7 in a caring place,
Forever to live, never more to die.

Now on that glad reunion day,
When the roll up yonder is called,
We'll gather in God's presence,
Praising Him one and all.

Be sure your heart is ready,
Make certain your soul is prepared.

For one day the angels to carry you,
To climb those Heavenly stairs.

It's only because of Jesus,
It's only through His precious blood,
That Daddy could move *from Room A7,*
To a home filled with nothing but love.

SCRIPTURE REFERENCES
Luke 16:22 ~ II Corinthians 5:8

AUTHOR'S NOTE

Written as a tribute to the memory of my "Daddy," **Ralph C. Flowe** *shortly after his passing.*

FULL OF GOD

So *full of God* I want to be
So blessed His presence to know;
But just how can that happen
Since He's everywhere I go?

The secret to being *full of God*
Is found through knowing and doing His will;
Empty yourself daily of what's taking His space
And let Him, with His goodness that fill.

Give His Spirit priority by spending time alone
Live moment by moment in tune;

Talk to Him, lean on Him, learn from Him -
You'll find yourself *full of God* soon!

SCRIPTURE REFERENCES
I Chronicles 16:11 ~ Psalm 63:6-8, 113:4-6, 19:11 ~ Isaiah 53:6
Matthew 6:33 ~ John 16 ~ Acts 9:1-6 ~ Colossians 1:9, 4:12 ~ James 4:8

GABRIEL BLOW YOUR TRUMPET

Gabriel, blow your trumpet,
For that sound I'm waiting to hear!
No sweeter sound I'm expecting,
Than when those notes fall on my ear.

Gabriel, when you blow your trumpet,
The dead in Christ will rise.
Those who remain will be caught up,
Together, we'll meet in the skies.

There Heaven bound forever,
Then too, Gabriel, will you play?
As all the saints march hand in hand,
Singing victory through amazing grace!

AUTHOR'S NOTE

Written during a Sunday night song service at Charity Baptist Church as
"Brother Bob" Bost, *now deceased, beautifully played on the trumpet,*
"When The Saints Go Marching In." I was reminded of I Thessalonians 4:13-18
which speaks of Jesus' return and of our leaving this world for better days.

GIVE SOMEONE YOUR KEYS

Oh no, is that a wreck?
I'm not sure, let me go check.
I run down the road...
The car suddenly explodes!
And I call 911…oh heck!
The ambulance arrives
Thank God that no one dies.
Say the driver was driving drunk?
What a serious thing
Will this, charges bring?
A good lesson should be learned:
"Put up the booze
Or your license you'll lose,
And seriously a life you might take."
So don't be foolish or dumb
When to driving it comes,
Watch out when the law you break.
You've gotta realize when you bring demise
Much more than your freedom is at stake...
Their life is in your hands.
So don't drive just 'cause you can,
Give someone your keys
Think of others, "Please, please!"

You don't want to live with blood on your hands -
Once a life is gone, it's gone!
So if you plan to drive drunk,
You'd better think it through,
And make other plans to get home!

———————⟨∞⟩———————

Give Thanks in Everything

Give thanks in everything
Everything, Lord???
In peril and danger
In famine and sword?

Yes, everything child
Trust what I say
In everything thank me
I'll show you the way.

Everything, Lord???
In sickness and pain
When it seems there's no way
It seems there's no gain?

Yes, everything child
There's victory to be found
When you give it all up
When you lay it all down.

Everything, Lord???
Those I don't understand
In family matters or messed up plans
When tragedy takes a loved one from my hand?

Yes, everything child
When your dreams fall through
Remember the plan is not all about you.

I'm not asking you to be thankful
For all things that are being done
I'm asking you to be thankful
Because **In all things** I can glorify my Son.

I have a way of mystery
You'll never fully understand
I'm asking you to **give thanks during all**
Trusting in my perfect plan.

SCRIPTURE REFERENCES
I Thessalonians 5:18

GOD IS UP TO SOMETHING

God is up to something.
I feel it deep within.
Although I can't explain it,
I'm at a place I've never been.
I feel His Spirit stirring,
Working faith within my soul.
I don't know what He's doing,
But I know He's in control.

He always has good things in mind.
He's proved it to me often.
When my heart has grown weary,
Its fibers He seeks to soften.
He always works to do me good.
He always seeks my best.
It's not that way with me alone,
All His children go through tests.

When we don't know the answers,
When we don't have a clue,
His will, He'll show, the way provide,
His love always proves true.

When *God is up to something*,
No greater love you'll find.
The peace and comfort given
Mortal man can not define.

SCRIPTURE REFERENCES
Jeremiah 29:11 ~ Romans 8:28, 12:2

GOD KNOWS WHAT HE IS DOING

Friend, *God knows what He is doing*,
Though, you may not think so.
He has it all within control.
He knows things that you don't know.
The future, present, and the past
Are His to rule and reign.
Control is His, though choices you make
And then will suffer consequences and pain.

He loves you like no other.
He gave His only Son.
He wants to see you happy
And to say to you, "Well done."
There is no other like Him.
There is but one true God.
He *knows what He is doing*
When at your heart He prods.

You may be full of questions
In the dark night of your soul.
Just keep this thought in mind, my friend,
Your God is in control.

He knows what He is doing.
His ways are not like ours.
He has a special plan for you
That Satan seeks to devour.

Don't let the devil steal your joy.
Don't let him come between you.
God knows what He is doing.
He can do what others can't do.
His grace will be sufficient,
He will make a way for you.
Cause *God knows what He is doing,*
And He'll always see you through!

SCRIPTURE REFERENCES
Isaiah 55:9 ~ Matthew 25:22-23 ~ Romans 11:33 ~ II Corinthians 12:9
Colossians 1:16-17

GOD'S GRACE

It's said, "*God's grace* is sufficient",
To get us through anything;
To take us through the deep water,
To our souls, relief it brings.

Known as God's unmerited favor,
We sure don't deserve it, that's true;
But I'm so thankful God in His great mercy,
Made salvation available to me and you.

In ourselves we cannot earn it,
It's God's riches at Christ's expense;

When Satan took charge of the souls of men,
Jesus came to our defense.

He laid down His life to atone for our sins,
Took our place and suffered our pain;
There's no other way for us to escape Hell,
No other name by which to be saved .

Yes, *God's grace* is a beautiful gift,
From our Heavenly Father above;
None can repay, none is worthy,
Of His endless, matchless love.

It's only by grace, through faith, that we enter,
Those beautiful gates of pearl;
"Amazing Grace, How Sweet the Sound",
We'll be singing as we leave this world!

SCRIPTURE REFERENCES
II Corinthians 12:9 ~ Ephesians 2:8-9 ~ II Timothy 1:19

GRACE, MERCY, AND PEACE

Grace, mercy, and peace
From God the Father and the Son;
The Spirit fills my soul today
As the three of them are ONE.

Grace, mercy, and peace
In unity they go;
Just like the three of the Godhead
With them my heart overflows

GRACE WILL GET ME THROUGH

On a cold day in December,
I heard the doctor say:
"The news I have to tell you
Is not the news I wanted for you today.

Your surgery indicated cancer cells
Within and without the "tumor."
Afterwards I called friends and family
Sharing details to avoid any rumors.

I'm trusting that God has victory for me.
I know He has ability to heal,
I'm believing Him for guidance now;
Grace will get me through this ordeal.

Like David, the Lord is my shepherd,
In the valley He restores my soul;
He **is** the Lily of the Valley,
By grace through faith I'm made whole.

SCRIPTURE REFERENCES
Acts 20:24 ~ II Corinthians 12:9 ~ Ephesians 4:7 ~ Hebrews 4:16

HALLELUJAH

Hallelujah, glory to God!
He gave the answers,
He gave the nod,
To set things in motion,
To work it all out,
He gets the glory,
My soul gives a shout.
Hallelujah, glory to God!
The victory has been won.
Hallelujah, glory to God!
Praise the Father, the Spirit, and the Son.

SCRIPTURE REFERENCES
Deuteronomy 6:5 ~ Colossians 3:17 ~ I Peter 3:15 ~ Revelation 5:13

HARD TIMES

God, you see my brokenness.
Jesus, you have felt the same.
Holy Spirit, you are my Comforter.
As the Trinity, you feel my pain.

Hard times have been good for me.
It's in those I know you care.
It's in the troubled times of life,
When I, the burden can't bear.

You tell me in your Holy Word
To cast my cares on you.

And when I follow your leading,
My spirit soars as renewed.

Joy comes in the morning,
only after the darkness of night.
As my brokenness is healed through love,
and my wounded wings take flight.

Hard times have been good for me,
Just like David in Psalm 119.
In times when my heart has gone astray,
through afflictions you cause me to sing.

Only because I have hoped in your Word
And know it alone speaks the truth,
And only because it's in the *hard times*
My soul better understands you.

SCRIPTURE REFERENCES
Psalm 30:5 ~ John 13:7 ~ I Corinthians 1:3

HE GIVES YOU LIFE

Just how much does God mean to you?
You say, you haven't stopped to ponder.
Well, think on this *He gives you life*,
And you won't need to further wonder:
He gives your lungs clean air to breathe,
He gives your heart blood to receive,
He gives you strength to get up and walk,
He gives you ability to think and talk,
He gives you food for energy,

He gives you eyes through which to see,
He gives you ears with which to hear,
He gives you five senses that bring good cheer.
All these things and so much more,
All these things you should thank Him for.
Just how much does God mean to you?
Without His power, know there's nothing you could do!

SCRIPTURE REFERENCES
Acts 17:28 ~ John 15:5

HE LEFT BEHIND

God sits on high in the heavens,
Ruling and reigning in power.
At the right hand of the Father,
Sits Jesus at this very hour.

The Holy Spirit beckons,
Men's hearts on Earth to fill.
It's up to us, each one decides,
If we will do His will.

God sent His little messenger,
On that first Christmas Day.
He grew in wisdom and stature,
The Light, the Truth, the Way.

He forsook everything so familiar,
To become **Immanuel**, God with us.
When He arrived if Earth had known,
We'd have made much more of a fuss.

He was born in humble surroundings,
Chosen parents loved and swaddled Him tight.
In a stable with shepherds as greeters,
All was changed in the course of one night.

He left behind the praise of angels,
To hear the cruel mockery of men.
No greater love was ever shown,
When He died to save us from sin.

He left behind a royal diadem,
In exchange for a crown of thorns.
But death could not conquer our Savior,
He arose early on that third morn.

He left behind Heaven's portals,
To bring salvation to me.
And "one day" when this life is over,
I'm certain His face I'll see.

SCRIPTURE REFERENCES
Matthew 1:23, 27:27-31 ~ Mark 15:31 ~ Luke 2:52 ~ Ephesians 1:20-23

HEALING HANDS

God grants wisdom to my doctors,
It doesn't come easy though;
Long hours they practice and study,
For those credentials on the wall to show.

I look at their hands as I visit,
I think Lord, what power they have;

To sever and sow and reconstruct,
To touch and mend as salve.

But Lord, I know and understand,
And hope all physicians do too;
No matter how much expertise they have,
You are the Great Physician -
And all healing comes from you!

You hold me in the palm of your hands,
What mighty hands are they!
For good health and restoration,
Lord, I look to you today.

So, I praise you Lord for healing,
The giver of life are you;
I gratefully thank you for my doctors,
Their lives have blessed my life anew.

The doctors who perform my surgeries,
Are the best that surgeons are;
But the hands that guide their hands I know,
Were bloodstained and are still nail scarred.

SCRIPTURE REFERENCES
Exodus 15:26 ~ Psalm 41:3,147:3 ~ Proverbs 2:6, 103:1-3 ~ Isaiah 53:4-5
Jeremiah 17:14 ~ Mark 2:17, 5:24-34 ~ John 20:25

HEART AND SOUL

One night at a little church revival,
The preacher spoke the words of God.
He reminded us all we were sinners,
On the road to Hell we'd trod.

Then he told how we could be forgiven
Through Jesus' cruel death on a cross.
Believe it, repent, get the victory,
Or forever in sin's grip be lost.

The words touched my heart as a young child,
The Spirit of God gained control.
Down at that old fashioned altar I prayed,
Giving Jesus my *heart and my soul.*

SCRIPTURE REFERENCES
John 3:16-17, 14:6 ~ Romans 6:23 ~ I John 1:9-10

———————— ∞ ————————

HIS AUTHORITY

The Creator rules all of Heaven,
His authority spreads over the Earth;
Whether it's admitted by all or not,
He initiates the seed of each birth.

Each fetus He sees from conception,
Beyond the darkness of the womb;
Each soul that has died and gone on,
Leaving mortal flesh in the tomb.

The spirit of man is the lifeline
That connects us to our maker;
Not only in birth and dying,
But the years in between known as "vapor".

From newborn baby to senior adult,
Things change and we go through life's seasons;
To acknowledge God and seek His wisdom,
Is vital for so many reasons.

SCRIPTURE REFERENCES
Ecclesiastes 3:1 ~ Jeremiah 1:5 ~ Matthew 28:18
I Corinthians 15:53-57 ~ Colossians 1:16 ~ James 4:13-15

HOLD ON

Hold on to the truths God's taught you;
Don't ever let them go.
Don't let anyone take what you have learned;
Those things have helped you grow.

It's not always been that easy;
Sometimes it's an uphill climb.
This world and its ways can get you down;
Sometimes there's no reason or rhyme.

When it all gets confusing and cluttered,
And your mind is a boggled mess;
That's when your faith and your trust in God,
Can really be put to the test.

Yes, *hold on* to the truths He's taught you;
Hold on to the Promises within.
The Holy Scripture provides for,
The falters and failures of men.

When you don't understand what's happening,
You're up to your neck in doubt;
Hold on your Savior knows every detail,
He'll save you and bring you out.

SCRIPTURE REFERENCES
I Corinthians 10:13 ~ II Corinthians 1:20 ~ James 1:2-4, 12
I Peter 1:7, 11, 4:12-19 ~ Revelation 3:11

HOW BEAUTIFUL ARE THE FEET

Had a visit from the preacher after surgery,
As he left he said, "Can I pray with you?"
In the circle I looked down at our feet
And saw his fine looking, black, dress shoes.

Right away, God spoke to my grateful heart:
How beautiful are the feet
Of those who spread the gospel
Of those who are called to preach.

A touch I felt from Heaven
As we gathered on that day.
I'll never forget the blessing and vision
Of my preacher's servant shoes as we prayed.

SCRIPTURE REFERENCES
Matthew 20:26 ~ Mark 10:42-45 ~ John 12:26 ~ Romans 10:13-15
Galatians 5:13 ~ II Timothy 1:9

———— ✺ ————

AUTHOR'S NOTE

*Written in honor of **Dr. R. J. "Beaver" Hammond and his wife, Faye**, who so faithfully continue inspiring & serving the body of believers while walking out the call of God in their lives.*

———— ✺ ————

I AM

I am **the Way, the Truth, the Life**
No man comes to God without me
I am your **Redeemer**, your hope for all times
Through my blood you can find victory

I am also called the **Good Shepherd**
I won't ever lead you wrong
Trust my hands to guide you daily
Know that when you're weak, I'm strong

I am the **Great Physician**
Go to the doctor, get his pills
Follow closely his good advice
But realize it's my power that heals

I am the **Lily of the Valley**
I am the **Bright Morning Star**
I'll be there through your darkest hour

As a reminder that I'm wherever you are

I *am* the **Bread of Life**
My touch your soul's hunger fulfills
When you seek me, you will find me
With satisfaction your longings I'll fill

I *am* the **True Vine** abide in me
Watch yourself begin to grow fruit
When you live out loud my glory to show
New believers will be reproduced

I *am* the **Alpha and Omega**
The beginning and the end
I *am* your **Refuge and Strong Tower**
Your soul and spirit I defend

To this dark world, I *am* the **Light**
Without me no one sees
The only way to get to Heaven
Is in my sacrifice to believe

I *am* the **Door**, the only way
To get to the Father above
Never forget how much we care
It was demonstrated through my life's blood

I *am* the **Resurrection and the Life**
Triumphantly on the third day was raised
Though your flesh may die, at the appointed time
You too will get out of that grave!

SCRIPTURE REFERENCES
Exodus 3:14 ~ Song of Solomon 2:1 ~ Isaiah 48:17 ~ Psalm 61:3
Mark 2:15-17 ~ John 6:35, 8:12, 10:9, 11-14, 11:25, 14:6, 15:1-8
Revelation 1:8, 22:16

Jesus is THE GREAT I AM. Whatever you need, HE is!

I Can

God, I can't do that...
Yes, child you can!
Because I am God,
And I made man.

Just let me do
The work through you.
You'll realize then,
"Hey, *I can* too!"

SCRIPTURE REFERENCES
Philippians 4:13

I Choose to Believe

I choose to believe you God,
Though Satan causes doubt;
I choose to believe you God,
When it seems there's no way out.

The key is in the words "it seems",
Because with you all things can happen;
When Satan's lies fall on my ears,
And my spirit he seeks to dampen.

I choose to believe you God,
You know just where I'm bound;
Just like the Israelites at the Red Sea,
On their heels those Egyptians were found.

Moses stood before the people,
Held his staff out and told them "Stand still";
Today you'll see the salvation of God,
With your enemy He'll surely deal.

The people crossed safely over,
On DRY GROUND all night they walked through;
They saw Almighty God fight their battle,
He did what He said He would do!

In the morning God's people were astonished,
Dead Egyptians washed up on the shore;
I choose to believe God you have not changed,
You can deal with the enemy once more.

Brave David stood before Goliath,
The soldiers all shook in their boots;
As the young shepherd boy cried out to the giant,
Big man you don't know the God of my roots!

You come to me with great weapons,
You have your shield and your sword;
I killed a lion and a bear with my hands,
I come to you in the name of the Lord.

Yes, *I choose to believe* you God,
Whatever the enemy might be;
You have not changed in you there's great power,
Over opposition, human, animal, or disease.

SCRIPTURE REFERENCES
Exodus 14:21-31 ~ I Samuel 17:1- 50 ~ II Kings 17:39

———⌒∽⌒———

AUTHOR'S NOTE

This poem was written very early in the morning on the day I was to visit my doctor to get results of the more intense testing of lymph nodes and tissues after mastectomy. I was already believing God for healing and thanked him openly in the presence of the doctor and his nurse when I heard the beautiful words, "There is no more cancer!"

———⌒∽⌒———

I Don't Know

I don't really know what my future holds,
Matter of fact, neither do you.
So why don't you put yours in the hands of God,
And see just what He can do.

He'll make of you a blessing,
Cause you to have more than enough.
He'll give you what you need,
Then he'll pile on more stuff.

If you will give to others
Of the bounty He has shared,
He'll make sure you have the means
To bless and show others that you care.

It's not about your glory,
It's not about a pat on the back;
It's all about uplifting His name,
He's the one who's keeping track.

It's not so you'll be rewarded,
But rewarded, you will be.
If you're in doubt, just step on out,
And then you will clearly see.

We can't buy our way into Heaven,
Trying to balance the scales of living;
It doesn't work that way, in balance we stay,
With pure motives of serving and giving.

If you give what you can,
Bless the souls of fellowman,
With motives pure and true.
I don't know what He does,
But I sure know this -
He'll send sweet blessings to you!

SCRIPTURE REFERENCES
Proverbs 11:24-25, 19:17 ~ Malachi 3:10 ~ Luke 6:38 ~ I Corinthians
10:31 ~ II Corinthians 9:6-11 ~ Ephesians 2:9-10, 20 ~ Philippians 4:19

I REST MY CASE

I plead my cause
I rest my case;
On the blood of Jesus
My life I've based.
There's no other plan
No other way;
Salvation came to Earth
That first Christmas Day.
Born of a virgin
Raised up in the flesh;
Born as a human
With humans did mesh.
He was born to die
For the human race;
God's ultimate plan
Satan sought to deface.
I plead my cause
I rest my case;
My name's in God's book
That no man can erase.

SCRIPTURE REFERENCES
Matthew 26:28 ~ Romans 3: 24-25 ~ Ephesians 1:7 ~ Colossians 1:20

I Want No Part

Whatever in the world would this world be
If love wasn't shared by you and me?
It seems there's less love these days to be found,
And I'm told love makes the world go 'round.

If love ends, will Earth stop spinning on its axis?
Will generosity and peace be "old hat"?
Well, it just might be, but I can surely say,
If there's no love, *I want no part* of that!

SCRIPTURE REFERENCES
John 13: 34-35 ~ Galatians 5:13 ~ Ephesians 4:2 ~ I Peter 4:8 ~ I John 4:16

I'll Take a Knee

Here alone, my heart begins to rejoice,
Lord, I'm so thankful I've made you my choice.

For all you've done for them and me,
I bow in praise to your sovereignty.

You worked things out according to your plan,
You gave your life to save the souls of man.

There's none so worthy as you Jesus,
Through eyes of love you look upon us.

Here all alone my heart begins to sing,
I bow in prayer my praises to bring.

Gratefulness floods my soul, so *I'll take a knee,*
Because Jesus you took the nails for me!

SCRIPTURE REFERENCES
Mark 15:1-39, John 3:16, 14:6, 20:25, Acts 4:12, Colossians 1:16-17

———————————∽∾———————————

IF GOD TELLS YOU

If God tells you to give it,
Somebody needs to have it.

If God tells you to say it,
Somebody needs to hear it.

If God tells you to do it,
Somebody needs it done.

Are you going to be obedient,
Will you be the faithful one?

SCRIPTURE REFERENCES
Deuteronomy 5:33 ~ I Kings 2:3 ~ Luke 10:27 ~ John 14:23 ~ James 1:22

———————————∽∾———————————

IF YOU LIVED LIKE YOU WERE DYING

If you lived like you were dying
Would you say that thing you said?
If you lived like you were dying
Would you speak words of peace instead?

Would you go about your business
With caring ways, more kindness show?
When family asked you to put aside your work
For fun, would you stop and go?

About fortune, fame, or getting ahead
Would you worry or fret so much?
Or would you slow down and think more of
The effect on the lives you touch?

Would you take time from your workload -
From the hassle of the modern rat race?
To call an old friend or acquaintance
Or stop to look your spouse in the face?

Would you finish that project you started
Cuddle up with a book and your child?
Stop and sit on a park bench observing
And greet passersby with a smile?

If you lived like you were dying
Do you think you'd give God more thought?
Of His plan and His power and His wisdom
Of the fact no more time can be bought?

His love for you is unending
He gave all He had that to show.

If you lived like you were dying
For sure, do you know where you'd go?

SCRIPTURE REFERENCES
Numbers 23:19 ~ Psalm 49:17 ~ Proverbs 15:1-2 ~ John 10:27-30
Galatians 5:22-23 ~ Ephesians 4:29, 32

IT'S A DEAL

"I'll make you a deal, how about it?"
The Devil says to me.
"I'll give you fame and fortune;
Just bow your heart and knees.

Serve me and I'll make it happen;
I'll give you all you need.
Happiness galore, good times evermore,
The best of it all, you will see!"

Oh, beware, when you've taken his offer,
And your life is on the line.
He'll turn it around, leave you there on the ground;
He'll give you no more of his time.

You're used up, he's had his way with you;
You're no good to him anymore.
He'll say, "Take your life, end it now, wretched soul;
Your dealer has walked out the door."

When you're low, and your heart is empty,
Turn to Jesus, He'll be waiting right there;
Look back, with eyes of faith and you'll see,

YOUR SIN on HIS CROSS He did bear.

You'll hear Him say, "How about it?
Are you ready to give up the fight?
Turn from sin, follow me, let me guide you;
Move from darkness into the light.

I'll give you my love unconditionally;
Inner peace and contentment you'll find.
If your heart you'll completely surrender,
I'll give you a renewed mind.

Forgiveness is what you are seeking;
It's all wrapped up in my Word.
You've been running from it far too long;
It's my grace so undeserved.

No one is truly worthy,
Of the sacrifice I made;
But with a humble heart, drop your foolish pride,
Because my blood for your soul I did trade.

I will make you worthy;
It's only through my death.
Live life with me, bow your heart and your knees,
And this new life will be your best."

"I see the benefits of salvation now, Lord;
You're right, I've been running too long.
It's a deal Lord Jesus, I'll follow you,
And look to You as you lead me on."

SCRIPTURE REFERENCES
Matthew 16:24-26, 26:14-16, 27:3-5, 32-50 ~ Romans 12:1-2
Ephesians 2:8-9

JESUS IS NO JOKE

Skeptics say this thing's not real,
That Jesus is just a joke.
Well, it sounds like they've never experienced
The Holy Spirit as He spoke.

When I knelt at an old time altar,
His Spirit let me know it was right.
Gave my heart to Jesus, made Him my Lord,
Hope I never get over that night.

Say Jesus is a joke if you want -
I choose to walk in His ways.
I choose to follow His guidance,
Trust His wisdom, and willingly obey.

If you could know what I know,
If you could see what I saw,
Then for real, you would more fully understand
Why on Him I confidently call.

So if you're one who likes to use that phrase,
Oh, I wish you'd open your heart
To see that there is a loving God,
And He'll meet you wherever you are.

If you could live what I've lived through,
If you could feel what I've felt,
And if you could go where I have been,
I believe on your knees you'd have knelt.

Truly, Jesus can be your dearest friend,
When you can't walk, He will carry you.
He's always there to share life's cares;
He promises to bring you through.

He knows about you what others don't know;
He'll forgive you of all your sins.
He'll go with you where others won't go,
Be your guide as your new life begins.

If you'd give Him the time of day,
Hear him as that night He spoke;
Allow Him to wrap your heart with his love,
Then you would know *Jesus is no joke!*

SCRIPTURE REFERENCES
Matthew 28:6 ~ Mark 8:27-29, 14:61-62 ~ John 8:56-58
Revelation 22:13

KEEP ME SWEET

"Keep me sweet and take me deep,"
I prayed to the Father one day.
"Lord, guard my tongue, help me watch my mouth,
I shouldn't say what I want to say!"

It's not always easy to live Christ-like,
To follow His perfect example,
To say what's on my heart and mind,
My vocabulary would surely be ample!

Words have power–they can sting like fire!
They live on in the memory.
But Lord, like I said, "It's my everyday prayer,
Take me deep and *keep me sweet.*"

I want to bite back, tell 'em just what I think;
They deserve it, if I let it roll.
But, I want to influence others for Jesus,
So my speech, I must learn to control.

SCRIPTURE REFERENCES
Psalm 19:4 ~ Proverbs 10:19, 15:4, 17:27-28, 21:23

———————∽———————

LET ME GLOW

Lord, *let me glow* for you today
As I walk the straight and narrow.
Let me glow for you today
As I walk down paths unknown.
Though I go through pain and sorrow
Let me glow through each tomorrow,
So that seekers may be able to see
There's something to that Jesus walk,
There's something to that Jesus talk.
Lord, *let me glow* for you today
So others may see something different in me.

SCRIPTURE REFERENCES
I Samuel 12:24 ~ Psalm 34:18 ~ Proverbs 4:18-27 ~ Acts 20:19
Ephesians 4:12 ~ Colossians 3:23-24

———————∽———————

LIFE IS SERIOUS BUSINESS

Life is serious business,
Each day countless decisions we make;
It's up to us the choice is ours,
Draw near to God, or get further away.

When we live according to His commandments,
We earn for ourselves peace of mind;
But when we turn our backs and disobey,
It brings suffering and failures we find.

When you're faced with powerful temptation
Or a difficult choice to make,
Remember *life is serious business* -
And there is so much at stake.

It's vitally important
To examine your ways and your words;
Because others your ways are noticing,
And your words good or bad are heard.

Take everything as it comes to you
With the idea this too shall pass;
Troubles surround each of us
But troubles, they never last.

Yes, *life is serious business,*
Each day we're hit with new things
That bring us worries or headaches
Or make our burdened hearts bleed.

There's pleasure in sin for a season,
But its sweetness will eventually turn sour.
Look ahead in wisdom and realize
It's your soul Satan seeks to devour.

Since *life is such serious business,*
And death is even greater still.
Will you take time to acknowledge
The seriousness of Calvary's hill?

SCRIPTURE REFERENCES
Matthew 20:20-28 ~ Mark 7:21-23, 10:35-45 ~ John 10:10, 13:34
I Corinthians 11:28 ~ Galatians 6:7 ~ Hebrews 2:3

LIVING WATER

I needed a drink of water,
So I went to the living well.
This water was oh, so different -
Miraculous I could tell.

It quenched my thirst immediately,
Unlike anything I've ever known.
As soon as I drank this *living water*,
An eternal seed in my soul was sown.

It brought on an understanding,
Peace like a Heavenly dove.
It brought on forgiveness and mercy,
Revealing an endless love.

Jesus is the *living water* -
He offers you, "Come drink, be filled."
From your sins and past be forgiven,
Drink of His cup, be forever healed.

SCRIPTURE REFERENCES
John 4…*(verse 10 specifically)*

———————∽———————

MASTER ARTIST

I serve a *Master Artist;*
The sky as His canvas is spread.
He lovingly paints the sunsets
In blues, purples, oranges, and reds.

Morning's breathtaking sunrises
Obviously are of his design;
No other could paint such a picture
More beautiful than His hand divine.

From a distance I view pretty flowers,
Their colors so vibrant and pure;
Then I move closer for a better look -
Ah, it's the Master's handiwork for sure.

When is the last time you lingered
To gaze at one's colors so blended?
For you to look at its beauty and see Him,
Is exactly what the *Master Artist* intended.

The designs and patterns of the animals -
Giraffes, zebras, tigers, a turtle's shell -

Display the highest level of artistry as in
Butterfly wings or a peacock's fanned tail.

To look upon His work so rare,
It ever thrills my soul!
My spirits rise and my doubts subside,
Knowing the *Master Artist* is in control.

SCRIPTURE REFERENCES
Psalm 19:1, 65:8

ME AND LAZARUS

Went to church one Sunday morning,
The preacher seemed like he was mad;
But then after I heard his sermon,
"I thought it the best warning I'd ever had."

After a while of stomping and yelling,
Flailing his hands in the air;
His words rang true, his heart showed through,
He taught things of which I was unaware.

He told us the story of *Lazarus*
And the rich man who lived so well;
How poor *Lazarus* had gone to Heaven,
But the rich man had gone to Hell.

Lazarus was taken to Heaven,
Escorted on angel wings;
He was no longer a beggar;
He partook of wonderful things.

The rich man cried out in torment:
"Just a drop of water, oh please!"
But too late, he never repented,
Upon God he never believed.

As I listened those flames got hotter,
I knew I was going there soon;
Conviction fell down, people gathered around,
As I said, "I want Jesus too."

Afterwards that old preacher approached me
And gave me a great big hug;
I knew then it wasn't us he was mad at -
But at Satan and his demon thugs.

SCRIPTURE REFERENCES
Luke 16:19-31, Romans 10:14-15

MEDICINE TO MY WOUNDS

Have you ever been wounded so deeply
That you felt you just might not make it?
Have you ever been wounded so deeply
That you felt you just couldn't take it?"

Well friend, I truly understand,
'Cause I've felt that way too;
But God in His mercy, love, and grace,
Reached down and carried me through.

He's no respecter of persons;
He loves us all the same.

Some of us love Him more it's said,
'Cause some have trusted His name.

IT'S THROUGH HIS PAIN we find comfort;
THROUGH HIS SACRIFICE there is relief.
It's only BY HIS DEATH ON THE CROSS,
WE FIND HEALING FROM OUR PAIN AND GRIEF.

The comfort of His sweet Holy Spirit,
Like a medicine to raw, deep wounds,
Is applied with divine intervention,
To keep our hearts attuned.

Scripture tells us, "Laughter is like medicine,"
Yet, if no laughter your heart can find,
Rely on the promises of His Holy Word,
As a balm for your soul and your mind.

SCRIPTURE REFERENCES
Proverbs 17:22 ~ Isaiah 53:3 ~ Acts 10:34 ~ Ephesians 2:4-5

MORE THAN ENOUGH

My preacher said if you take care of God's business,
He'll take care of yours.
If you give as you should and love as He would,
Sweet blessings your giving secures.

God can bless you with everything you need,
You will always have *more than enough.*
To give of your time, your talents, and resources,
As in His provision you obediently trust.

More than enough to do kind things,
More than enough to share with others.
If you do what's right, as God guides and provides,
You too will receive from sisters and brothers.

Give, and it shall be given unto you
If your motives are pure and true.
Don't worry if you give it all away,
God promises to give it all back to you.

SCRIPTURE REFERENCES
Exodus 36:3-7 ~ Proverbs 11:24-25 ~ Luke 6:38 ~ II Corinthians 9:6-13
Hebrews 13:6

MY ADVICE

Expand your knowledge, broaden your horizons,
Spread your wings each day.
Help somebody, give a smile,
And continually grow in grace.

Believe in yourself, don't trust your doubts,
Know you can do anything.
The sky is the limit, no boundaries place,
Give your soul a song to sing.

Always consider others,
Wear their shoes, send some light their way.
Help them know, when the sun's not shining,
There's still hope of a brighter day.

Days sometimes don't turn out,
The way you had envisioned;
But when you hear that still small voice,
Make sure to give a listen.

It's not always a good idea,
Just because your brain gives notion.
Better think that through,
Just because your mind told you,
Doesn't mean it's as deep as the ocean.

Make sure to weigh the words of others,
Some things are true, some are lies.
When you feel at the bottom of the barrel,
Remember cream will always rise.

There is a master plan for you,
It was drawn a long time ago -
By hands that seek the best for you,
From a heart that you should know.

Don't live your life haphazardly,
You should truthfully consider -
Your ways, your days, your attitude,
'Cause life can squeeze you till you're bitter.

Don't let your thoughts go all over the map,
Settle down, know what you believe.
Build yourself a firm foundation,
Don't let yourself be deceived.

I'd say you need to think for yourself,
Not everything is right for you.
Unless God said it, then don't bet on it,
'Cause it just might not be true!

SCRIPTURE REFERENCES
II Samuel 7:28 ~ Psalm 94:19 ~ Proverbs 16:19 ~ Ephesians 4:25-27, 29
Romans 12:3 ~ I Peter 3:10-12 ~ II Peter 3:18 ~ James 1:22

MY CONSTANT COMPANION

I need my family
I need my friends
But at the surgery room doors
Their companionship ends

They pray for me
Their thoughts go too
But only one companion
Can see me through

God's sweet Holy Spirit
A presence so divine
He will never ever leave me
He's with me all the time

Yes, it's God's sweet Holy Spirit
With me when others aren't around
From *my constant companion,*
No greater comfort can be found

SCRIPTURE REFERENCES
Deuteronomy 31:6, Hebrews 13:5

My Life Is in Your Hands

You gave me life at conception,
It was all plotted out in your plan.
From the start of my life till its ending,
I know I've been held in your hands.

Troubles, trials, or great tribulations,
They come upon us all.
But when they come upon me,
On your great name I can call.

In joy I look to you Lord,
In sorrow or distress.
You're the only one who can help me,
When my life gets in a mess.

In days of peace and comfort,
When all seems to go well.
My life is in your hands then too,
Either way of your goodness I'll tell.

SCRIPTURE REFERENCES
Psalm 18:6, 29:11, 50:15, Isaiah 49:14-16

My Soul Cries Out

I am so weak;
I cannot speak.
What should I say?
Who'll hear anyway?

My words not uttered,
My heart is aflutter.
What has caused this?
It's a deep abyss!
My soul cries out to God alone;
For my sin, His death atoned.
He was so weak;
He could barely speak.
His love ran red;
As His Spirit fled.
Today with Him, my soul communes;
He feels my pain, My Savior true.
He holds my heart in His loving hands;
As no one can, He understands.

SCRIPTURE REFERENCES
Isaiah 4:10 ~ Luke 23:46 ~ II Corinthians 12:8-10 ~ Hebrews 4:14

New Growth

Walked outside one late winter morning,
Saw buds forming all around...
On cherry trees, Bradford pears, and forsythia,
To become flowers those buds were bound.

Upon further inspection, it was noted,
Leaves and stalks were popping out of the ground.
The showers had been so frequent,
It's a wonder their bulbs hadn't drowned!

With the welcomed, warm rays of sunshine,
With the much needed rhythm of the rain,

The look of my garden was changing,
From its growth, there was no refrain.

From their cold winter's deep, dark domain,
Saw red tulips and golden daffodils rising.
In a few more weeks much to everyone's delight,
Those bulbs would bring a colorful surprising.

Trailing down the wheelbarrow was sedum,
From the walls hung creeping jenny,
Variegated vinca traveled over the mulch,
My "ground cover" ornamentals were many.

I saw creation serving its purpose,
Evidence of *new growth* everywhere could be seen,
Then I prayed, "Lord, create a hunger and thirst,
Grow the seed of faith in me."

SCRIPTURE REFERENCES
Genesis 1:11-12 ~ Psalm 89:11 ~ Luke 17:5 ~ Acts 4:24
Colossians 1:9-10 ~ II Peter 3:18

NEW MERCIES

His mercies are new every morning
Because we use each day's supply;
He looks on His children with favor
As the apple of His eye.
His grace is promised to be sufficient
And I've found that is the case;
Each year of my experience
This truth I've been able to trace.

Yes, His mercies are new every morning
But mercy never comes to an end;
Because I used up yesterday's supply
For today, *new mercies* He sends.

SCRIPTURE REFERENCES
Deuteronomy 4:31 ~ Lamentations 3:22-23 ~ Ephesians 2:4 ~ Hebrews
4:16 ~ I Peter 1:7

ODE TO PAYTON: I'LL LOVE YOU FOREVER AND A DAY

I'm sorry for the pain you're feeling,
And that I left you behind to stay.
All our friends and family are so happy here;
We've laid down our robes of clay.
It's so beautiful in this country;
In Jesus, we all rejoice.
You're all just gonna love it here too;
Keep on listening to His sweet voice.
My challenges and struggles are over;
Those worldly things have passed.
One day, you too will join us,
When you have breathed your last.
The happiness that I found on Earth,
Gives nothing to compare,
To the joy up here and the peace of mind,
There is nothing like it down there.
I'll see you real soon and I'm waiting;
I'm doing just fine, I'm OK.
Until then lean on Jesus and remember,

"I'll love you forever and a day!"

AUTHOR'S NOTE

Dedicated to the loving memory of our precious, young family friend, **Payton Denise Furr,** *who suddenly left this world for her Heavenly home. One of her favorite sayings to those she loved as they were parting was,* **"I'll love you forever and a day!"**

OPEN YOUR WINGS

Beautifully delicate butterfly,
Never seen a creature like you;
You lift fragile wings and take off in flight
Soaring up toward the skies so blue.

I watch you as you flit and flutter,
Awestruck at what I see;
You move with such grace and glory
As I watch, God's voice speaks to me.

Child, you also are beautifully delicate,
There's no one on Earth just like you;
If you *open your wings* and trust me
You'll find yourself free to fly too.

You're fragile and weak in your own strength,
Your skies are limited by doubt;
Look unto me and take courage in knowing
Faith in me moves your wings up and out.

Yes, I'll take you higher than ever,
I'll be the wind beneath your wings;
Don't be afraid to follow my lead
By my grace you can do mighty things.

If your wings get heavy with raindrops,
Don't just sit around and cry;
Flit and flutter and shake them all off
Spread your wings and then you can fly!

AUTHOR'S NOTE

Inspired to compose this poem during what Satan intended to be a soul defeating time in my life. God spoke softly to my spirit saying, "Open your wings and fly; you can't fly until you open your wings." I perceived Him to be planting in me the same thoughts as are in Philippians 4:13....I can do all things through Christ who strengthens me. I find peace and tranquility in watching and taking pictures of the butterflies that are drawn each spring and summer to the flowers I plant especially for them.

PEACE BEYOND UNDERSTANDING

There's *peace beyond understanding;*
It's a peace not everyone knows.
It comes from a trust deep in your heart,
Of going where not everyone goes.

Troubles, trials, heartaches, and grief,
They come to us all, everyone.
The thing that brings peace in the difficult times,

Is a relationship with God's Son.

We all go through stuff, it's for certain;
This life can really pour it on.
But the difference in the way that some go through,
Is that some, don't go through it alone.

There are usually friends and family to cry with;
There are cards, books, and texts to read.
But when friends and family aren't with us,
There's a great friend, the best friend, indeed!

Look to Him when uncertain of where else to turn,
When life makes no sense at all.
Look to Him when you're on your knees in pain;
He hears you when you call.

While prayers for peace and comfort,
That many others are praying for you.
This *peace beyond understanding,*
Comes daily, as it you pursue.

Seek God, lean on Him, trust His wisdom;
Yes, hurting you still will be.
But when you call on Him, with a longing heart,
This calmness your soul will see.

Through eyes of faith in His sovereignty,
Through trust that for now brings great hope,
A heart satisfaction coming only from God,
When you're at the end of your rope.

The Bible speaks of this sweet peace,
Describing it in this way:
It's *peace that passes understanding,*
Causing you to realize, it's gonna be OK.

That loved one cannot return from the grave;
That straying one may stay astray.
The times might get tougher, the bills may get higher,
But don't let yourself be dismayed.

No, it's not crazy to believe it;
Things may get better, they may not.
But believe I will, trust in His Word still,
Since this peace to my heart He has brought.

SCRIPTURE REFERENCES
Numbers 6:24-26 ~ John 14:27 ~ Philippians 4:6-7

PRAYER

Do you believe in the power of prayer,
Or are those just words you're repeating?
If you have confidence in God's might,
Your prayers can be worry defeating.

The effectual fervent *prayer*
Of a righteous man availeth much;
It's clear that you can expect results,
When intensely, Heaven you touch.

Your prayers are so important,
Simple even though they may be;
God listens to your utterances,
Oh, He listens attentively.

Just call on His name in thankfulness,
Believing the best you'll receive;

Open your heart to trust His will,
No begging or wordy prayers you need.

Sometimes saying, "Oh Lord, I need you"
Sometimes "God help me as I call,"
There are times when the burden is so heavy,
No words will come at all.

Sometimes you feel the need
To pour out your heart and your fears;
And even though the pain is great,
God can still read your tears.

There are times when you just feel better
Telling Him all, everything;
He's got the time to listen
When emotions are in full swing.

Some days you don't know what to ask for;
At times, you ask for foolish things;
In His wisdom He doesn't give them,
Because of heartbreak He knows they will bring.

Maybe the timing is not ready,
Maybe your heart's still not right;
Maybe you're not even thankful,
For things already in your life.

So pray and seek His counsel;
Do what you feel is right;
Then wait on Him to work things out,
Knowing His ways are good and kind.

Yes, *prayer* is of great importance,
Through it God should also be praised.
It's good to enter His throne room,
With a grateful heart and your hands raised.

He knows every little detail,
He has it all under control;
By *prayer* one touches the hem of His garment,
It can soothe the weary soul.

You show your faith when you call on Him,
And faith is what moves His hand;
He knows everything before you ask,
The heart and needs of every man.

SCRIPTURE REFERENCES
Jeremiah 33:3 ~ Matthew 6:6-8 ~ Philippians 4:6-7 ~ Colossians 4:2
James 5:16

Purpose, Plan, and Presence

I know there is a *purpose*
I know there is a *plan*
I sense an awesome *presence*
While being held in those nail scarred hands.

Your *plan* is to redeem me
You love all mankind the same
My *purpose* is to serve you
To honor and glorify your name.

Your Spirit makes your *presence* known
As I trust you I know it's so real
You long to be my comfort and guide
And cause me your *presence* to feel.

SCRIPTURE REFERENCES
Psalm 16:11, 37:23, 46:10, 57:2,145:18 ~ Romans 8:28

REFLECTIONS

"*Reflections* of my *journey*"
Are seen through the eyes of time;
And when I look back, I realize
There was an unseen hand holding mine!

I can see His hand of mercy
I look back to a plan not known;
Not that He didn't know the plan
But that to me, His plan wasn't shown.

It seems that it is best that way
Too many surprises good and bad;
If I'd have known what was to be
I might have spent too much time being sad.

So my motto has become as the saying goes:
"Just take life one day at a time;"
And when I reflect on my *journey*
I'll say, "Thank you God for your hand divine."

SCRIPTURE REFERENCES
Psalm 89:13-15 ~ Lamentations 3:22-23

Rest

Child, *rest* when you're weary
Rest when you're faint
Rest when I can
Rest when you can't

Come unto me
In me, *rest* you'll find
Not the "lay me down to sleep"
But the "peace that passes understanding" kind

SCRIPTURE REFERENCES
Matthew 11:28-30, Philippians 4:6-7

Reveal

Lord, will you *reveal* your love through me?
Show your mercies anew
So that, by my witness here below
My life will speak to a few.

Reveal the work that you have planned
Those tasks before ordained;
So as I go, I can safely say
I've done works in Jesus' name.

SCRIPTURE REFERENCES
John 9:4 ~ Ephesians 2:10, 4:12 ~ Philippians 2:13 ~ Colossians 1:10, 3:17

RISE AND SHINE

Rise and shine you've heard it said,
What is that all about?
Rise and shine get out of bed,
Don't let your light go out.

Talk to God and fervently pray,
Let others see His light in you.
Rise and shine start out your day,
Bless God in all that you do.

Rise and shine even when it's dark,
All around you and others don't care.
Rise and shine draw souls to him,
By the love and the light you share.

Of course, there's always those gray days,
when you're down and your fuel needs renewed.
Lean on God let him pick you up,
It will encourage others to *rise and shine* too.

It's not always easy to stay afloat,
'Cause nothing goes right all the time.
Look deep within and bring that light out,
That's what's meant by *rise and shine!*

SCRIPTURE REFERENCES
Psalm 119:105 ~ Isaiah 60:1-3 ~ Daniel 12:3 ~ Matthew 5:15-16
John 1:14 ~ II Corinthians 4:6 ~ Galatians 4:22-23

Sin

There is pleasure in *sin* for a season,
The Bible has proved this is true.
When the Devil appears with temptation,
Remember you are responsible for you!

Yes, he makes it look good in your eyesight,
He'll tempt you with all of his might.
Use your brain, take a stand, think of Jesus,
Even though it is hard, do what's right!

God rewards those who seek to follow
In His ways, His path, His truths.
Sin always has a big bill to pay,
Remember you are responsible for you!

SIN IS: <u>DOING</u> WHAT YOU KNOW IS WRONG or
<u>NOT DOING</u> WHAT YOU KNOW IS RIGHT*

SCRIPTURE REFERENCES
Numbers 32:23 ~ Deuteronomy 6:18 ~ Hosea 14:9 ~ Romans 6:23-24
I Corinthians 10:13 ~ Titus 2:11-14 ~ Hebrews 9:28 ~ *James 4:17
I John 1:9

SPEAK LORD

Speak Lord, I want to hear you,
I'm about to start my day.
Speak Lord, I want to hear you,
As I strive, to walk the narrow way.

Yearning to feel your presence,
Lead me as I go.
I seek to shine as a glowing light,
So that other souls many know.

You are the source of all things good,
You are the Creator, who sustains.
Speak Lord to my hungry soul,
Lead me to the greater gain.

Speak Lord, I want to hear you,
Guide me on my daily walk.
Speak Lord I want to hear you,
I'll be silent as you talk.

Speak Lord I seek to hear you,
I'm here to get direction.
Speak Lord, I seek to hear you,
I want to stay, with you, connected.

Speak Lord, I want to hear you,
It's you who has the wisdom and power.
It's you who knows my right from wrong,
You see my future, from hour to hour.

I long to journey side by side,
As we walk in one accord.
As I live in this sin cursed world,

Getting strength from your living Word.

I'm here because I trust you,
And I know you know it all.
I'm here because I love you,
On your holy name I call.

Into your throne room this morning,
Fall before you as I enter.
Speak Lord, I'm waiting to hear you,
Around you, my attention is centered.

I hear you and I'm waiting,
To know the things you know.
I'm here to seek your face,
So I'll know which way to go.

So, *speak Lord*, I'm ready to follow,
Not my will but yours.
Speak Lord I want to stay on your path,
Complete my assignment and bravely endure.

SCRIPTURE REFERENCES
Matthew 7:13-14 ~ John 15:5 ~ Hebrews 4:16 ~ James 4:8 ~ Revelation 4:11

STEP BY STEP

Step by Step
Day by day
Lord, you're with me
All the way.
I hear your voice

I sense your touch
You hold me tenderly
In your strong clutch.
You say to me,
"Child do not fear
It's by your side
I'm so very near."
I feel a sweet calm
As you walk beside
Lord, you're my shepherd
My constant Guide.

SCRIPTURE REFERENCES
Joshua 1:9, Psalm 37:23

STRENGTH TO MY SPIRITUAL BONES

FAITH is the great upholder
Giving strength to my needy frame;
Faith comes only by hearing,
Hearing of God's Word proclaimed.

PRAYER gives support and courage
It makes me feel all is well;
When friends call and say they are praying,
My fears and doubts it dispels.

GRACE comes on quietly covering
My soul, bringing peace and rest;
I know deep within I can feel it,
Through grace I will pass this test.

Faith, prayer and grace are like partners
Making my inner man strong;
Bringing comfort, hope, and assurance,
Giving *strength to my spiritual bones.*

SCRIPTURE REFERENCES
II Corinthians 5:7 ~ Hebrew 4:16 ~ James 4:6, 5:16

TAKE CARE

As we part from each other
And go our separate ways,
"Take care," you say to me,
It's a very common phrase.

But what exactly do we mean,
When those words cross our mouths?
Well, I'm not sure, what they mean to you,
But, around here in the South,

We're saying be mindful of what you do;
Be kind to your body, feed it well.
Don't work yourself into the ground;
Take time to sit a spell.

Be careful of how you talk and act;
Someone's always watching you.

Don't judge others, don't be so mean,
And to thine own self be true.

Watch yourself, watch out for others;
The world is full of evil.
Don't let yourself walk away from God;
Don't make friends with the Devil.

"*Take care* now, till we meet again;
I hope to see you soon.
Take care now, my dear friend,
Till the next time we commune."

SCRIPTURE REFERENCES
Proverbs 1:7, 12:15 ~ Psalm 141:3 ~ Mark 6:31 ~ Galatians 5:22-23
Ephesians 5:15

THANK YOU GOD

Thank you God for using me
You've given me a desire,
To serve you and to live for you
To spread the Gospel's fire.

It's not the power within me
Because truly I have none;
It's through the Holy Spirit's work
Through belief in your only Son.

So God whatever you've put inside,
Let me bring it out for your glory.
So all my days I'll sing your praise,
And share your part of my story.

SCRIPTURE REFERENCES
Psalm 34:1-4, 35:28, 95:2-3, 103:1-6 ~ Micah 6:8 ~ Mark 16:15
1 Corinthians 7:17 ~ Philippians 2:13

THE BEAM

Come here, in your eye a speck I see,
Let me get it out, 'cause it's bothering me.
Don't you feel it, can't you see it too?
If you don't then, something is wrong with you.

You ask me how I'm doing,
I say I'm doing fine;
And that's because I usually do
Things right most all the time.

Let me help clear your thoughts my brother,
'Cause you've got stinkin' thinkin';
If you think you have no faults,
Your mind in deceit is sinkin'.

So, maybe you'd better stop and reconsider,
Although self righteous you seem;
Somebody needs to set you straight,
'Cause in your eye there's a big *beam*.

Don't judge me till you look within,
Question your own motives and your heart;
You might just find when you take out that *beam*,
Your vision was blurred from the start.

SCRIPTURE REFERENCES
Matthew 7:1-5 ~ Luke 16:15 ~ Philippians 2:3 ~ James 4:10

———————⟨∞⟩———————

THE BOOK OF LIFE

Every life is like a book
With chapters known as years;
Every year is divided into months
With days that quickly disappear.

Those days are filled with minutes
That pass with the blink of an eye;
Those minutes are divided into seconds
And it's all considered time.

Every "book" has a beginning
As well, each has an end;
But the contents of the pages in the middle
On each person those greatly depend.

Each page of a book is filled with words
That make the storyline flow;
They give the reader understanding
They take the mind where the narrative goes.

Each author has a direction
They want their work to take;
Our creator also has a good plan
Of His will for each to partake.

Every sentence has punctuation
To separate words and to clarify;
Each life has stop and go times
Sometimes known as the "seasons of life".

Just like the plot in a mystery
A book is full of the element of surprise;
Of periods, question marks, exclamations
Life also, is comprised.

Each "book" is written by the minute
With times of happiness, ho hum, and drama;
We never know just what to expect -
So never put a period where God has put a comma,*

SCRIPTURE REFERENCES
Ecclesiastes 3:1-8, 12:7 ~ Romans 14:8 ~ James 4:14 ~ Jeremiah 29:11
Revelation 21:4

AUTHOR'S NOTE

*Famous comedienne, Gracie Allen, near the end of her life penned these
words in a love letter to her husband, George Burns.*

The Bright and Morning Star

One night as I went walking,
I looked up at the sky.
The stars were brightly shining,
But one star caught my eye.
More than all the others glistening,
Their lights on Earth to shed,
My thoughts flowed to the Bible,
And what of Jesus it said.
He is *"The Bright and Morning Star"*,
The one whose light gives life.
The one who for me the ransom paid,
He died to make things right.
I'll never leave or forsake you.
I'll be there when others have gone.
I remembered His vow of faithfulness,
As I stared at how brightly the star shone.
The first one to draw your attention.
The last one to leave from your view.
It's true, He's *"The Bright and Morning Star"*.
Let the light of His love shine through you!

SCRIPTURE REFERENCES
Hebrews 13:5 ~ II Peter 1:19 ~ Revelation 22:16

AUTHOR'S NOTE

Diagnosed with breast cancer four days prior to writing this poem and was inspired while walking early one morning to clear my head and talk to God. Very few stars out but the morning star was very obvious.

THE CHRISTIAN LIFE

Living *the Christian life*
Is really a big deal.
Maybe you need to think more on that,
If that's not the way you feel.

The time you have to influence others
Is sometimes only given one shot.
Yes, living for Jesus is a big deal,
Don't ever think it's not.

Some things we handle easily,
Some things we flow through as a breeze.
Other events hit us harder,
As we're gut punched down to our knees.

Get mad and pout or stay puffed up,
Or get over it, show love, and move on.
Your choices have much to do with
How you're remembered when you are gone.

Spend time with the Savior
Fueling up for life's race.
While praising Him and thanking Him,
For sacrificially taking your place.

Seek and then trust his counsel
No better advice could be given.
Walk in His ways and obey Him,
And *the Christian life* you'll be living.

SCRIPTURE REFERENCES
Psalm 51:10, 128:1 ~ Galatians 6:14 ~ Philippians 2:8 ~ Colossians 3:13
Hebrews 10:22

THE DIFFERENCE IN MY DAY

Got up this morning
Hit the ground **running**
"My, there is so much to do!"
Gotta get it all done
Gotta be there for that
Gotta see and talk to who's who.

Went about my day
On my merry way
With an attitude kinda grim.
Didn't pay attention
To souls that were searching
Didn't give much thought to Him.

Got up this morning
Hit the ground **praying**
"Lord, there is so much to do!"
Need your help with this
Need your wisdom in that
Gonna do for you what I can do.

Want to go about my day
Walking in your ways
With an attitude of dependence.
Trying to pay attention
To souls in spiritual detention
Living life as you intended.

Got up this morning
Hit the ground **praising**
Saying "Where would you have me to go?"
I'm so greatly blessed
As I enter into your rest

Spirit tell me what I need to know.

Want to go about my day
Doing things your way
With an attitude of praise.
Compelled to pay full attention
While seeking your intervention
And my soul Heaven's anthems to raise.

Whichever attitude I wake with
Makes *the difference in my day,*
Whether walking in my flesh
Or walking under the Spirit's sway.

SCRIPTURE REFERENCES
Psalm 100:1-4 ~ Philippians 1:27, 4:8-9 ~ Colossians 3:23-24

THE FLAME

Holy God, light a fire within me,
With the oil of your Spirit let it burn;
Like smoldering hot coals in a fireplace,
Let my soul for your presence yearn.

The oil and the winds of your Spirit,
Understanding and wisdom they bring;
Let me grow to have greater attachment,
To your cross let me always cling.

Not just a believer who lives for
Religious rules and regulations;
But one who lives for the glory of God,
And in the joy of my salvation.

If in time, my passion wanes,
And my love for you grows cold;
Reignite *the flame* of devotion,
Protect me from the enemy of my soul.

Lord, anoint me with consecration,
Bring your wise thoughts to my mind;
Let me feel that kindred spirit,
With brothers and sisters in the tie that binds.

Empower me with your Holy Spirit,
To do the work, you have "called" me to;
I abide, I am indwelt, I am joined with Jesus,
For your will to fervently pursue.

When I would go astray lead me back into the way,
As a shepherd who leads his sheep;
You are my Savior, the one true God,
And you promise that my soul you'll keep.

Sweet Spirit of God I'm depending on you,
I'll fan the spark that starts the flame;
As I go on in life, and with all my heart strive,
To bring honor to Jesus' name.

SCRIPTURE REFERENCES
Psalm 42:1, 86:12 ~ John 13:34-35, 15:1-12 ~ Romans 12:5
I Corinthians 10:31 ~ II Timothy 1:6-7

THE KEYS

After Jesus gave His life,
On that cruel, bloody cross,
In authority, He recovered,
Valuable things that were lost.

The keys to eternity,
Death, Hell, and the grave,
Were all regained forever
Through the sacrifice He made.

The priceless, precious blood
That He shed of His own free will,
Has power to save, offers liberty today
And provides forgiveness still.

As real as it was
On the day that He died,
That freedom exists,
Through the scars in His side.

The keys He recovered,
Through the torture He endured,
Give hope to the soul,
An eternal anchor that is sure.

He invites us today,
To open our heart's door and let Him in.
His death is the only key
For new life to begin.

The key to Heaven He now holds
In suffering He obtained it.
The key to your heart you control;

Be wise and don't retain it.

His unconditional love for all,
Is what unlocked the way.
Life and hope and joy and peace
Are yours when you obey.

SCRIPTURE REFERENCES
Isaiah 52:14 ~ Mark 15:24 ~ John 8:36 ~ Romans 6:22 ~ II Corinthians 3:17
Ephesians 6:12 ~ I Peter 2:24 ~ Revelation 1:18, 3:20

THE PEACE OF GOD

God, I know by myself I can't do this,
Walk with me holding my hand.
I feel so restless and uneasy,
Till I sense you helping me stand.

Whatever it is that happens,
Whatever comes my way,
I'll remember that you can handle it,
And that I should bow and pray.

I know your Word informs me,
That I can experience *"the peace of God"*;
That only comes from involving you,
Then my heart and mind it will guard.

This matter controls my thinking;
By your grace I want to realize,
The peace that transcends what I can feel,
Heartfelt but not seen with my eyes.

I ask for wisdom and freedom from worry,
For needed strength to go through;
This *"peace of God"* that others speak of
I believe I can have it too.

SCRIPTURE REFERENCES
Philippians 4:6-7

THE ROCK

All of us face those storms in life
Is your house built on *the "Rock"*?
If your foundation is Jesus
Your faith and His will, interlock.

The sinking sand will fail you
But on God's promises you can rely.
Make sure your house is built on *the "Rock"*
You'll still have troubles but grace He'll supply.

SCRIPTURE REFERENCES
Psalm 40:1-2 ~ Matthew 7:24-27 ~ Luke 6:46-49

THE SHEPHERD KIND AND TRUE

The little lamb kept straying
Until there came a day,
When he looked all around him
And found he had lost his way.
He had wandered from the shepherd
Thinking all would be OK.

But then, his eyes were opened
The green pastures were no more in view,
The little lamb had wandered far
From *the shepherd kind and true.*

As he looked all around him
The clear, still waters he craved,
He cried out for his master
The only one with power to save.

He spent long nights in the valley
Darkness fell cold, no comfort he found,
But then one day upon his ears
The shepherd's voice was the sweetest sound.

He spoke to the lost lamb so gently
With love his wounds were bound,
Then the shepherd tenderly picked him up
On his shoulders carried him around.

His was the heart of compassion
Understanding the little lamb's need,
For days on end he nurtured
Planting in him a loving seed.

There is a beautiful lesson
In the lamb that went astray,
For when the shepherd put him on the ground
He never again lost his way.

He stayed close by the shepherd
He longed to hear his voice,
He could have wandered off again
But to stay close was his choice.

From all the days of hurting
Through all the nights of pain,
The little lamb had realized
In straying there was no gain.

To follow the ways of the shepherd
He realized would be best,
Because in the shadow of the shepherd
The sheep truly find sweet rest.

SCRIPTURE REFERENCES
Psalm 23, 28:8-9, 91:1, 100:3, 116:4 ~ Proverbs 14:14, 24:16
Jeremiah 8:5,14:7 ~ Galatians 4:9 ~ John 10:1-5, 25-30

AUTHOR'S NOTE

Inspired by a wooden plaque that says "THE LORD IS MY SHEPHERD." It was one of those hard days when I was asking God for direction, wisdom, and words concerning a very difficult relationship challenge on "MY JOURNEY." The minute I prayed, "God, please tell me what to do", my eyes fell on those words hanging on my kitchen wall. I sensed Him saying, "LET ME BE YOUR SHEPHERD." I totally understood that He wanted me to gain comfort in knowing that He would take me to the places I needed to go, give me words to say, and provide for me as I went, just as a kind loving shepherd does for His sheep. PTL!

THE TAPESTRY OF LIFE

I was given a colorful tapestry
To hang upon my wall;
After admiring it's great beauty,
Turned it over and then I saw...

On the backside there was no picture,
Only scribbly lines of yarn to view;
As I thought of the sight I was seeing,
I thought about me and you.

Our lives are much like a tapestry,
Woven deliberately by unseen hands;
We don't have a clue what tomorrow holds,
That backside is just like our plans.

We think we have it all together,
Knowing how our days should look;
But then things change and it all goes awry,
Like tearing a page from a book.

Our lives at times seem to be a mess,
Oh my, how can this be true?
We feel like a tattered old rag doll,
Feeling as though our lives are through.

You say, the ugly backside of the tapestry,
Is not the bright future I saw;
This muddle of color doesn't make sense,
It's not going at all how I thought.

Then turning from that side of the tapestry,
To study more closely it's front;
A greater picture begins to unfold.
And the valuable lesson to be learned.

Right now we don't see the whole picture,
Only after all is said and done;
Do our lives reveal magnificent patterns,
As the *tapestry of life* is spun.

When we can't see His hand at work,
We must learn to trust His heart;
He sees our lives from beginning to end,
We humans aren't that smart.

We don't understand the pricking,
Or the prodding as the yarn pulls through;
We can't see tomorrow, so it's best to trust
That the master weaver has good plans in view.

SCRIPTURE REFERENCES
Proverbs 3:5-6, 16:1-4, 9, 19:20-21, 25:3-6, 27:1, 86:11 ~ Jeremiah 29:11
II Corinthians 4:17-18 ~ Philippians 1:6

THE TRAINING OF THE SOUL

There may come a day in your own life,
Where you find no hope of relief.
The things that happen to you,
May bring sorrow, death, and grief.

None of us knows his *journey*,
Until his *journey* is past.
None of us knows the future,
Just that good times do not last.

Bad things happen to good people,
We've often heard it said,
But we can't live in the present,
With fear, regret or dread.

We must trust God with our future,
Only He knows what lies ahead.
If we put all our trust in others,
We'll at some point be misled.

Troubles and trials are His method,
Of developing a heart for Him.
He trains the soul through suffering,
Polishing the sufferer into a beautiful gem.

A treasure to be used for His glory,
Demonstrating the sufficiency of His grace,
Qualifying us for our "calling,"
Creating a need to seek His face.

The school of suffering can be brutal,
Whatever the cause may be,
But the hours and the days of training,
Will bring rewards for eternity!

If we allow the Father to teach us,
School ourselves to be patient and learn,
While obediently seeking to be in His will,
We'll receive peace, love, and joy in return.

How long is *the training of the soul*?
Much of that you must decide.
Will you allow Him to train and mold you,
Take your soul through the pain of this life?

Learn some amazing things about yourself
Learn to listen to the voice of God.
Trudge through tall mountains and deep valleys
Walk lonely paths your weary feet will trod.

There's great beauty in *the training of the soul*.
I believe it's God's perfect intent,
To train us to become more Christ like,
When our time in this school is spent.

SCRIPTURE REFERENCES
Proverbs 4:1-13 ~ Luke 6:40 ~ II Corinthians 1:25, 9:24-27, 12:9
Hebrews 5:11-14

AUTHOR'S NOTE

God brings loving discipline to our lives and uses our sinfulness and mistakes as would a good teacher or a good Father, to help us learn from them and mature spiritually because of them.

THE VEIL OF HOPE

Hope is the anchor of the soul;
It keeps the ship of life steady.
When despair comes along to steal sweet peace,
And burdens cut like a machete.

There is a veil mentioned in the Bible
Separating the two parts of the temple;
In one section all worshippers could gather,
But in the other only priests could enter.

The second section was called the Most Holy,
Representing the Earthly presence of God.
Signifying God's and man's separation by sin,
Only high priests were to pass beyond.

On the cross when Jesus said, "It is finished,"
Cried to the Father, and gave up the ghost;
The thick veil of the temple was torn in two,
That veil being much thicker than most.

It was also very high and sturdy;
Human hands could it not have torn.
The way was made open for all to enter in,
Through the nails and the crown Jesus wore.

He made a way for us to enter,
Into the presence of the Heavenly Father.
Only through his precious blood,
Are we made priests, sons and daughters.

We have hope of our redemption,
We have hope of eternal life;
That hope is not as wishing for
A new car, or a house, or a bike.

Jesus followers are on a promised *journey*,
It's a hope his death and resurrection made certain.
Through our trust in his sacrifice to save,
And the revelation God gave in that curtain.

SCRIPTURE REFERENCES
Psalm 119:114, 130:5 ~ Matthew 27: 50-51 ~ Mark 15:38 ~ Romans 15:13
Hebrews 6:19, 9:11-12, 10:19-23 ~ I Peter 2:5

THE WILL OF GOD

Is the *will of God* important to you?
What does God want? What's His plan?
He has good in mind. He knows what is best,
But He will not of you demand,

That you follow His will,
Or that you walk in His way.
If you choose not to,
You don't have to obey.

It's all up to you.
A robot you're not.
The ability to makes choices
Is a gift we've all got.

Because of His great love,
He won't force your hand.
It's been our decision
Since the creation of man.

But it's you who will miss the blessing.
It's you who will incur the cost.
It's you who will find in the long run,
The best things in life were lost.

If you choose to live life your own way,
Not giving much thought to His Word,
Thinking the truths of the Bible,
Are only foolishness and absurd.

Before your life on earth has ended,
Before your time for judgment is near,
Be sure you've thought about this,
On the cross God made His will clear.

SCRIPTURE REFERENCES
Micah 6:8 ~ I Timothy 2:3-4 ~ Hebrews 13:21

TIME TICKS ON

It was in the wee hours of the morning,
And I was all snuggled in bed.
My husband had his arm on my shoulder;
His watch was ticking at my head.

As the seconds rolled on I thought of
How moment by moment we live;

That none of us knows the number of our days
Or the time to each our Maker will give.

It's true, our lives are like a vapor,
Like fog or a thick heavy mist;
For only a short while compared to eternity,
Does our *journey* through this life exist.

Second by second we live it,
Those seconds turn into our days;
Will you be happy with the way you've lived,
When your body and your spirit part ways?

Time ticks on, life flies by
While you're busy doing all sorts of things
Will you be prepared when your time comes
To meet the King of Kings?

SCRIPTURE REFERENCES
Psalm 90:12-17 ~ Acts 1:7 ~ II Corinthians 6:2 ~ James 4:14 ~ II Peter 3:8

TRUE SERVANTS

True servants of God know they're nothing,
Without God they can't do a thing.
Oh, there's plenty of stuff they can accomplish,
But without God, no value those bring.

True servants know and they realize
How insignificant they are.
Just like a jail or a prison
Is no good without the bars.

It's the grace of God working through them,
Bringing about His will.
That's what makes *true servants* special -
They desire His purposes to fulfill.

SCRIPTURE REFERENCES
Psalm 127:1 ~ John 15:5 ~ I Corinthians 15:10 ~ Ephesians 6:6-7

TRUST, REST, AND ENDURE

Was awakened early one morning,
Felt wounded, found myself in great pain;
The things I heard brought devastation,
Found myself in a cloud of black rain.

Although I didn't want to,
Was hearing, my world was falling apart;
Couldn't believe the conversation,
As words gripped the strings of my heart.

Quickly ran to my Heavenly Father,
He's the source of all comfort I know;
Lord, tell me the way, lead me in it,
Your guidance and wisdom please show.

"Trust in me," was the first thing He told me.
"You won't get there in your strength alone;
Look to me, this takes time but I'll take you,
To a place where your soul will have grown.

It took years on that emotional roller coaster,
Of heartache, soul searching, deep pain;

Someone I love even told me,
"Your life will never be the same!"

Dug deeper than ever into scripture,
Clung to His promises with all of my might;
There were many long days of struggling;
There was weeping that went on all night.

"**Rest in me,**" was the next word He gave me,
"Cast all your heavy burdens," He said;
"Satan will bind your mind with worry,
Bog you down with great fear and dread!"

"Your past will be the present,
I'll gift to you my child;
If you will rest in obedient faith,
But be patient, it will take a while."

"Although it seems this is mostly about you,
I must consider all people involved;
'Cause I not only care for you, my child,
But to see everyone's self dependence dissolved."

"This battle is based on my purposes,
Although sinful nature brought it about;
My will and my ways were never considered,
For I was totally left out."

"Now I'm dead set in the middle,
Which is where I want to be;
Your eyes to open and their eyes too,
So now, all eyes are on me."

"**ENDURE,** keep on fighting the good fight,
Your humble prayers keep lifting to me;
Keep looking to Heaven, keep waiting and longing,

As desires you express on your knees."

"I hear you, I see you, I know it,
Nothing goes unnoticed in my plan;
It's all to bring out obedience and faith,
Once it's over you'll more fully understand."

"So *TRUST, REST, and ENDURE* my child,
As you go about your days;
The more you do, the more I'll reveal,
Of my perfect, unexplainable ways."

"The future has never been yours to know,
Those mysteries belong only to me;
But the more you *TRUST, REST, AND ENDURE,*
The more of them, I'll let you see."

While the months and the years pass slowly by,
Growth and reliance are experienced each day;
I find myself no longer pitiful but powerful,
As confidence in my Lord is gained.

When finally, the heavy, gray clouds part,
A ray of sunshine falls on my face;
I look toward the skies with a thankful heart,
Brought through the fires by amazing grace.

He gave me beauty for ashes,
Traded lonely paths of sorrow, I'm free;
Took my barrenness and broken pieces,
Turned them into great joy and sweet peace.

"Now, remember what I have shown you," He said,
Remember the things you've been taught;
Not only for you but for others,
This miracle has been wrought."

"Not for your show, but for my glory,
  Not for your honor, but for my praise;
  Not to make you look good in mans' sight,
  But to lift up my name all your days."

"Encouraging others with the comfort,
  Your Heavenly Father gave you;
  Teaching them to lean in and grow in grace,
  As they *TRUST, REST, and ENDURE* too."

SCRIPTURE REFERENCES

TRUST: Psalm 9:10 ~ Psalm 28:7 ~ Proverbs 3:5-6 ~ Jeremiah 26:3
REST: Exodus 33:14 ~ Psalm 23:2-3 ~ Psalm 62:1-2 ~ Psalm 73:26
           Isaiah 40:29-31
ENDURE: Romans 15:4 ~ I Corinthians 13:7 ~ Hebrews 10:36
           James 1:2, 4 ~ I Peter 2:19

U TURN

Lord, U *turn* mourning into laughter
U turn sadness into dance
U work good things for those who love U
For them, nothing happens by chance.

U turn dark clouds into sunshine
Give us hope for the days ahead
U turn uncertainty into confidence
When on slippery slopes we tread.

Lord U know our every weakness
U know the mind's defeat
U turn unresolved situations

Into resolved ones and relief.

U turn the hearts of others
Toward myself, your plans, and U
U bring reconciliation along the way
When relationships are askew.

U give peace that passes understanding
It's the kind Earth can't afford
It comes by trusting in your hand
By believing your inspired Word.

U turn ashes into beauty
Where a heap is all we see
U put our brokenness back together
When all that remains is debris.

U turn disease into remission
U turn sinners into saints
U help us with the things we can
U do the things we can't.

Lord, surely there's no other like U
U turn our everlasting destination
From a sad forever filled with pain
To eternal life in your Holy Nation.

SCRIPTURE REFERENCES
Psalm 30:11 ~ Isaiah 61:3 ~ Luke 1:37 ~ Romans 6:23, 8:28
II Corinthians 12:9 ~ Ephesians 4:32 ~ Colossians 1:20-22 ~ I John 5:14

Unfinished Business

One day as I was riding
In the car back from the beach,
I saw a sight in a half plowed field
That a lesson to my soul would teach.

A tractor sat right in the middle
Of a field with not much left to go,
Till the farmer would have been finished
Preparing the ground for another crop to grow.

I wondered his reason for quitting
When I saw the tractor just sitting;
To have made a few more circles in his field
To complete the plowing seemed more fitting.

Did he get called home for "supper"
By a tender, loving wife?
Or did he get bogged down and have to stop
Due to some other cares of life?

Did he have to attend a funeral
Did he get tired or sick?
Were there other chores more important
Ready crops that had to be picked?

Was it time for recital or practice
Was his child in a school play?
Did it start out to be real pretty
Then turn into a wet, soggy day?

Maybe there was an emergency
Maybe he got a sad call.
Could be he just got real thirsty

And there was no problem at all.

Time could have possibly run out
It could've just gotten dark;
For whatever the reason was
That big green John Deere sat parked.

He may have been mentally exhausted
The tractor could have just run hot;
Or maybe he ran out of fuel
And it caused the engine to stop.

He might have heard nature's call
Or just plain got too sleepy.
What if he died or got badly hurt
Oh no! That would be freaky.

Why did the farmer leave his field?
What was this person's reason
Still having this *unfinished business*
Right in the middle of planting season?

It's true, I don't know what happened
But it sure made me stop to think;
Why were the few rows of his field left unplowed
And of the *unfinished business* I've got to complete?

SCRIPTURE REFERENCES
Job 12:1-6, 14:15 ~ Psalm 39:4, 90:10 ~ James 4:14

WALLS

We build *walls*; some *walls* are small.
We build *walls*; some *walls* are tall.
Why would we build a *wall* at all?
Walls are for keeping some things in
And for keeping some things out.
For whatever reason, have you built a *wall?*
Are there people you don't care for at all?
Have hurt and anger laid the bricks?
Have words and bitterness carved the sticks?
The stones of names that you've been called
What would happen, if you let it fall?
Would your days be happier if you gave up the fight?
Would an apology help to put an end to the strife?
Then who's to be first? What are you waiting for?
Take love's hammer to that *wall;* bust open the door!
So they still won't let you in, you say,
Neither wants to drop foolish pride;
Well, if you don't soon tear it down...
Too late, cause one of you will have died!

SCRIPTURE REFERENCES
Ecclesiastes 4:26, 7:9 ~ Matthew 6:14-15 ~ Mark 9:50 ~ Romans 12:18
II Corinthians 1:11 ~ Ephesians 4:31-32 ~ Colossians 3:8 ~ I Peter 2:1

WELL DONE, MY CHILD

Are you laying up treasures?
Are you waiting on His call?
One day the trumpet of God will sound;
Gabriel will summon for us all.

When you stand before the Master,
Don't you want to hear him say:
Well done my child, you've served me well;
Enter in, you're here to stay?

Here is your robe, your shoes, and a ring,
A glittering crown with Jesus to share;
For all that you've done in my name,
While you were walking down there.

You've fought the good fight and kept the faith,
Your race on Earth has been run;
Come on in dear child, you're home at last -
Forever with the Father, the Spirit, and the Son.

SCRIPTURE REFERENCES
Matthew 6:19-21, 25:21 ~ Luke 15:22 ~ John 3:3 ~ Romans 6:23
I Thessalonians 4:16 ~ II Timothy 4:7

———————⸺———————

What a Day Brings

What in the world can a day bring?
Bright sunshine, blue skies, summer rain.
It all seems so beautiful and you're happy...
But then, comes the dark clouds of pain.

In a moment a storm can start brewing,
Before the blink of an eye.
Fear can grip your heart like a razor,
Held close to your throat in the night.

It's no telling the things that a day brings;
That's why it's important you see,
To start out your day with thanksgiving,
Prayer and praise are always the keys.

You can't plan for the situations a day brings;
Some may give great joy and glee.
You never know what your future holds;
Some days might take you down to your knees.

You may fall in the floor with laughter,
Or you may be down picking up pieces.
Either way, His Word heals the hurting soul,
And His compassion never ceases.

His mercies are new every morning,
His unconditional love is beyond compare.
So, *whatever a day brings* cannot destroy you,
If you bring your burdens to the ONE who cares.

SCRIPTURE REFERENCES
Psalm 37:5, 55:22 ~ Lamentations 3:22-23 ~ I Peter 5:7 ~ I John 3:1

WHAT'S NEW

I met an old friend and as we crossed paths
He said to me, "Hey there, *what's new?*"
I said "Brother, if you've got a minute
I'll spend it sharing with you.

You remember how we would drink and carouse
With good buddies and good timin' women?
Well, things have changed, I've found the Lord
Now it's a new life I'm living.

I never put much thought into
The destiny of my eternal soul.
But one winter night, I was invited to church
And I went 'cause I wasn't feeling whole.

Through the years, circumstances and tough situations
Had caused my eyes to stay dry.
But that night as the preacher spoke God's Word
I felt myself begin to cry.

I really couldn't believe it,
That tender tug on my heart I felt.
As they began to sing that closing song
At that old fashioned altar I knelt.

I prayed what they call "The Sinner's Prayer",
Inviting Jesus into my heart.
When I got up, from off my knees
I knew, I was given a new start.

So friend, you know I love you,
We've known each other quite some time;

I'd like for you to be in Heaven with me,
But you've got to make things right.

You can't do it on your own
To admit you're a sinner, you must.
Let the Spirit of God soften your heart
As in Jesus, you put your trust.

He died on the Cross to save us all
As John 3:16 clearly says,
Whosoever believes in Him
With salvation will be blessed.

So friend, understand there's no pressure,
I'm speaking out of love and concern.
I've read the Bible now and I understand
Without forgiveness from God, souls will burn.

It won't be quick as a matchstick,
Forever and ever many souls there will be,
Forever and ever in torture
Yes, for all eternity.

I love you, so I'm trying to warn you
Of all the lost sinners' plight."
Then my friend who was under conviction
Gave his heart to the Lord that night.

SCRIPTURE REFERENCES
Matthew 10:28, 25:41 ~ Romans 3:22-24, 6:23 ~ Ephesians 2:8-9
Hebrews 9:14 ~ II Peter 2:4

WILLING BUT NOT WORTHY

LORD, I'm *willing but I'm not worthy*
To do a work for you;
I'm *willing but I'm not worthy*
To do what you've called me to do.

You've put in my spirit this gift -
The gift of song or speech;
You've given me a heart for this
To minister, play an instrument or teach.

To serve in administration,
To lead or to organize,
LORD, I'm *willing but I'm not worthy*
My abilities are precious in your sight.

You have wired each of your children differently,
To accomplish good things for your glory:
The call to preach, a calling to encourage,
The gift to explain your story.

A desire to aid in helping others,
The gift of service or that of giving,
A desire to bless sisters and brothers,
To impart knowledge and wisdom for living.

A heart to comfort others
In their time of need,
The gift of showing mercy and compassion,
Of exhortation or of hospitality.

The gift of showing kindness,
Meeting needs or of prophecy,
The gift of showering others with love

Or encouraging unity.

To you, I make myself available,
My goal is your kingdom's growth;
Since I love, honor, and respect you,
I'll trust and follow you, both.

Your atoning sacrifice gives me victory,
It's through nothing that I have done;
LORD, I'm *willing but I'm not worthy -*
I'm made worthy through the blood of your son.

SCRIPTURE REFERENCES
Matthew 5:16 ~ Romans 12:48 ~ I Corinthians 12:4-12, 15:10
Galatians 2:20 ~ Ephesians 4:11-16 ~ Philippians 2:13 ~ Hebrews 13:21
I Peter 4:10-11

WINGS OF FAITH

I'm praying for you
Those words I hear,
Spoken by many
Who to me are so dear.

Words uttered in prayer
Rise on *wings of faith,*
The second they are spoken
They arrive in the throne room of grace.

The Father not only listens
To each heart cry and each word;
He also recognizes each voice

Of the child that is being heard.

Prayer then opens the door
So to your heart He can speak,
As you intercede for others
Or for His will you seek.

SCRIPTURE REFERENCES
Psalm 55:17, 145:18 ~ Matthew 7:11 ~ John 15:7 ~ Ephesians 2:18
Philippians 4:6 ~ Hebrews 4:16 ~ James 5:16 ~ I John 5:14

WITH GOD

Why would you say, "It's impossible"?
If you do, there's something you don't know:
My God is a God of miracles,
And His power He's willing to show.

He's able and I firmly believe it,
To do exceedingly, abundantly, above all,
I can think or ask or imagine,
When in faith, on His name I call.

With God, nothing shall be impossible;
Scripture tells us on that to rely.
Those words, when my confidence was fading,
Caused hope in my heart to survive.

Say whatever you want and believe it;
I choose to believe that He can.
I've seen Him work in my circumstances;
I've seen Him change the heart of man.

I've seen Him do great things for me;
What others cannot do, He can.

"It's impossible"? Ok, you believe that;
I know better, I've learned from the past.
If God did it once, He can do it once more,
To that fact my soul will hold fast.

It may be something that I've never seen,
That I've never asked him for.
He's my provider, Jehovah Jireh
He's my Savior, my King, my Lord.

With God, all things are possible,
So I ask Him to make a way.
He answers, delivers, and leads my soul,
To a happier, much brighter day.

Don't tell me it's impossible;
I won't hear it, I've heard enough.
I've seen God move, seen His glory fall,
By now, I've already seen too much.

You might as well forget it,
'Cause you can't change my mind;
My God is true, my God is faithful,
His ways are so good and so kind.

Though I may not understand Him,
His ways I cannot see;
I'll trust His heart, I'll live by faith,
He's proved His love to me.

It may make no sense to others;
"Give it up, forget it", they say.
But I will cling to what I can't see;

On the impossible, I'll patiently wait.

SCRIPTURE REFERENCES
Genesis 18:14 ~ Exodus 34:6 ~ Numbers 23:19 ~ Job 42:2
Matthew 19:26 ~ Luke 1:37 ~ Romans 4:21, 8:28, 11:33 ~ II Corinthians 9:8
Ephesians 3:20

WITH HIM, THROUGH HIM

Do you know what to do when you can't?
Do you know the ONE who can?
If you can't, then He will;
If you won't, then He can't.
You can do all things *through Him.*
He can do all things through you,
Without Him, you are nothing.
With Him, all things are possible.
All things are possible with Him.

SCRIPTURE REFERENCES
Psalm 37:5 ~ Matthew 19:26 ~ Romans 8:37 ~ Philippians 4:13

Would You

Loyal, royal king *would you*
Breath is us your life?
Light your spark of greatness
And in our souls ignite,
A fire that forever carries
A torch for generations,
An all consuming flame of love
That spreads to all the nations.

That still small voice within us
Urging us to leave the world outside,
Causing us to bow before you
Dropping the robe of foolish pride.
As we look all around us
We can see the day approaching;
Guide us Lord on that narrow road
As your kingdom we're promoting.

SCRIPTURE REFERENCES
Job 33:4 ~ Psalm 1:1-3, 145:4 ~ Proverbs 4:10-27
Matthew 6:33, 28:18-20 ~ Luke 1:50 ~ II Corinthians 5:20

Wounded Warrior

I'm a *wounded warrior* trying to fight
To trust your will, to do what's right.
It's never easy when the battle rages
The demons of Hell are loosed from their cages.
They whisper their torments of doubts and fears

Lord, with your Word, let me block up my ears.
I've hurt for some time with constant pain
Wondering will I ever be the same again?
No, because your will is for me to grow
To become more like Jesus, His suffering to know.
Spiritual growth happens when I die to the flesh
Lord, help me today as I'm put to the test.
There's a gaping wound only your touch can repair
You said you'd bring comfort and my burdens share.
I love you today with a passion that's strong
Keep my mind from thinking thoughts that are wrong.
The chains of the past have my spirit bound
Break me free Lord, as I bow to the ground.
I'm a *wounded warrior* still trying to fight
Trusting your will, trying to do things right.

SCRIPTURE REFERENCES
Psalm 9:10 ~ Jeremiah 17:7-8 ~ Mark 8:35 ~ John 12:24 ~ I Corinthians 1:3
II Corinthians 1:3 ~ Galatians 2:20, 4:22-24 ~ Philippians 3:13-14

Your Faithfulness

Use me, Lord; infuse me, Lord;
Prove me, day by day.
'Cause Lord, I've proven You,
And found You faithful in every way.

When I think I can count on others,
Sometimes they let me down.
But Lord, I know I can count on You;
Sometimes no one but you can be found.

You show me love and mercy,
Bring fulfillment to my days;
I have no one I trust like You,
You are faithful through every phase.

When responsibilities and relationships
Lay heavy on my mind,
When the world seeks to betray me,
It's in You true faithfulness I find:

You seek to do me good Lord,
You are faithful in all your ways,
You will never forsake or desert me,
You'll give guidance through all my days,

You are steadfast and committed,
Your unconditional love stays ablaze,
You are dedicated and dependable,
For *your faithfulness* I offer praise.

SCRIPTURE REFERENCES
Romans 8:31-39 ~ II Thessalonians 3:3 ~ II Timothy 2:13
Hebrews 10:23, 13:5

Your Spiritual Bank Account

If you need money from your bank account,
And a check you plan to take,
Then make sure you've made enough deposit
Of funds that amount to make.

Each life has a *spiritual bank account,*
So when you need some knowledge,
It's best to seek the face of God
His kind doesn't come from college.

Memorizing verses in the Bible,
Believing its promises are really true,
Used to reawaken hope in someone else
Or bring comfort and strength anew.

When someone you know needs wisdom,
It's the teachings of Jesus you should heed,
By adding to your *spiritual bank account*
You will have whatever you need.

The Word tells us to lay up treasures,
Unlike cash, it can't be taken away,
Your Heavenly bank account keeps growing
With interest compounded each day.

SCRIPTURE REFERENCES
Proverbs 2:6, 16:16 ~ Matthew 6:19-21 ~ Colossians 4:5-6 ~ James 3:17

YOURS OR MINE

Each spring in my front porch fern basket,
Purple finches build their nest;
They fly back and forth on mini trips,
Creating a home for their eggs to rest.

One stormy night the wind showed muscle,
And the nest began to sway;

The oak leaves stirred and the broom straw rustled,
I hoped my baby birds would be ok!

From inside my home, I began to worry
About the tiny creatures outside;
As I peered in the nest thinking, "Oh my goodness
How on Earth can these gusts they survive?"

So I took down the basket, carried it to safety,
With thoughts that all would be fine;
When suddenly I heard the Lord speak to my heart
Saying, "ARE THESE BIRDS *YOURS OR MINE?*

Did you have anything to do with building their nest?
What about their hatching, anything with that?
Getting the chicks to this point in life,
To your credit can this you add?"

"Well Lord, I guess you said it,
It's a negative to all three;
Their birth and their growth and their current situation
Has had nothing to do with me."

"So then child, why would you worry?
Put the basket back in its place.
Leave their care to me; I can take it from here;
Let your mind no more fears embrace."

When morning came and the bright sun shone,
Ran outside to take a look;
Took down the basket and pulled back the fronds,
Remembering how violently their little house shook.

The basket seemed fine so the outlook was good,
Dark clouds vanished and so had the rain;
I was so happy when I peeked inside,

To find my little buddies still looked the same.

I lifted that flowing fern basket,
Hung it right there on the hook;
Went back inside to start my day,
Pondering the care our creator took.

"Dear Lord, I should've known better,
I'm sorry for my doubt;
You know that I was so concerned -
Was just trying to help you out.

A beautiful lesson I've learned from this,
You've driven it home I believe;
If you can take care of those tiny feathered fellas,
Then you can surely take care of me!"

SCRIPTURE REFERENCES
Genesis 1:1 ~ Deuteronomy 10:14 ~ Nehemiah 9:6 ~ Job 41:11
Matthew 6:26 ~ Psalm 24:1-2, 89:11, 104:10-14, 24-25 ~ Acts 4:24
I Corinthians 10:26

Good for the Soul

GOOD FOR THE SOUL

The life of every human consists of body, spirit, and *soul*. This section contains poems that relate to the *soul*, which is the presence that causes our physical body to exist as we are today and then continues to live on, forever after death. It serves as the mediator between the body and spirit, where the two meet. Belonging to the physical world and the spiritual world, it shares both of their characteristics. The *soul* is our personality, the intellect, the self-consciousness. It is who we are and is composed of our mind, will, and emotions...controlling our thoughts, choices, and feelings. It is the element of our humanity that allows us to reason, make decisions, and remember. The *soul* fuels one's desires and affections. It also determines our interactions with others as well as our perception of situations and people.

The function of the *soul* is to keep the spirit and the body in the correct relationship to each other. As God intended, it is to express in life and bring out in love the God within us. Since our choices are controlled by this part of our being, we can lean more toward either the spiritual realm or the physical realm. This choice creates the battleground of the mind which includes good and evil. God in his goodness has given us the right known as free will to decide how we live.

———————————

Genesis 2:7 ~ Deuteronomy 4:29 ~ Joshua 22:5 ~ Psalm 19:7, 23:3, 42:1, 62:1,103:1 ~ Proverbs 16:24 ~ Jeremiah 6:16 ~ Matthew 10:28, 16:26, 22:37-38 ~ Mark 8:36 ~ Luke 1:46-47, 9:25 ~ II Corinthians 5:6-8
I Thessalonians 5:23

———————————

A Friend Like You

There are people out there who are hurting,
Some are heavy hearted and blue;
There are people out there who are longing,
To have *a friend like you.*

A friend they can trust with their thoughts and cares,
A friend with whom life's burdens are shared;
Everybody's looking, whether they reveal it or not,
Everybody needs good friends sent from God.

To have a friend, one needs to be a friend,
Someone others can count on and trust;
Someone to call up and share good news,
When to spill it, they're about to bust.

A friend who'll speak the truth in love,
Someone to be just and fair;
Another person, another shoulder to cry on,
Someone to show how much they care.

Life is filled with blue skies, then rain,
Life is filled with laughter, then pain;
If you have a true friend you can call your own,
Then you know in your heart, you'll never walk alone.

SCRIPTURE REFERENCES
Proverbs 18:24, 27:9, 17, Ephesians 4:15

A Hug

I need *a hug*
Oh can't you see
A hug from you
Will do wonders for me.
Arms wrapped in arms
What caring it shows
Nose next to ears
Hearts all aglow.
So give me *a hug*
Spread some good cheer
I feel so much better
When you are so near.

A Mouse in My House

There's *a mouse in my house*
Oh Lordy, get a broom.
It's for certain for the two of us
There's just not enough room.

I scan for him every second
Catch a glimpse of him once in a while.
But to live with *a mouse in my house*
Is simply not my style.

With my screaming and my swatting
I try to coax him to go outside.
With my jumping and wide eyed motions

It seems I've lost my mind.

Sorry, but I can't stand it any longer
I must set a sticky trap.
Well good, now he's a goner
Let's call this drama a wrap.

A POET

Can you pen words and give them rhythm?
Can you place words where they will rhyme?
Can you write verses that click with timing?
Can you hear music in your every line?
Can you stir up imagination
With vivid language that creates fascination?
Can you provoke deep thought with repetition,
Adding phrases in just the right position?
Using your perception to build depiction,
Creating in the mind a mental description;
Can you drum up some common stanzas,
Using what you know to sow understanding?
Can you come up with some sensible jargon,
Something that sets thoughts right on target?
Can you write down some good sounding terms,
Till it's complete in your mind, your poem burns?
Can you plan a pause with correct line breaks?
Sounds to me then, you have what it takes.
Do you hear poetry in your sleep?
Words coming to you that you rush to keep?
Write them all down before you they leave,
So if them from your mind you can't retrieve;

Listen to the pauses, patterns, and timing,
Making sure the end result is all aligning.
This gift you've been given is from Heaven above
To benefit others and promote God's love.
Once your words are heard, they'll surely know it,
And then you can rightly be called *a poet*.

A SPECIAL BLESSING

So many of you have been praying,
You call and tell me so,
Or you give me a hug and whisper:
"Let us know how everything goes."

Your calls, cards, and notes overwhelm me,
I read as from the mailbox I walk,
Warm tears flow as I'm reading,
Then God and I have a talk.

Lord, thank you for friends so faithful,
Some of them praying don't even know me,
But the power in prayer, and the force of it all,
Are some things in which we believe.

So God, I ask you a favor,
That on all them who've thought much of me,
You give *a special blessing*,
That they'll know came straight from thee.

A True Friend

A friend will love you at all times,
Just exactly what does that ensure?
That they won't necessarily like all you do,
But that *true friendship* will endure.

It means they'll walk through thick and thin,
Sowing compassion when times get lean.
When you are hurt but don't say a word,
Their senses are sharpened by the unseen.

When you fall on your face, they'll pick you up,
True friends with heartstrings are bound.
It doesn't matter the circumstance,
They'll show up for whatever's going down.

It means they will stand beside you,
When you're out in the pouring rain.
You'll find them holding your umbrella,
While they also are feeling your pain.

When you're feeling down, wearing a frown,
Need some sunshine for your soul.
They'll be the one to bring out the smiles,
To make your half a whole.

True friends walk beside you down paths unknown,
Face the blackest nights and deep shadows.
Share the fun of lighthearted conversations,
Hear your heart in those things that matter.

True friends won't desert you,
Even when the times get tough.
They will stay in the battered boat with you,

When the winds and the waves get rough.

With you they're happy to engage
In all sorts of things you might plan;
Be it goofy or serious it might even be,
Just to lend a helping hand.

Friends show love and mercy,
In whatever they choose to do.
Whatever color your sky is,
They're always gonna be "true blue".

Though buried deep beneath a garment of flesh,
Their sincere heart you will always see.
When constructive criticism is needed,
And feelings are worn on the sleeve.

Know in your heart when you're not very smart,
When you've chosen foolishly...
That a *true friend* will guide you back to the path,
On which God wants you to be.

When you look around, no one else can be found,
Your faults and failures they cover.
Then you'll know in your heart a *true friend* you've found,
A companion like gold you've discovered.

There are times of giving opinions,
When eye to eye you don't see.
But *true friends* give you that freedom,
And will allow you to disagree.

A *true friend* sees in you,
What others do not see.
What is *a true friend* you ask?
Well, it's what you are to me.

SCRIPTURE REFERENCES
Proverbs 17:17, 27:5-6, 9, 17 ~ Ecclesiastes 4:9-10 ~ Romans 12:10
Colossians 3:13

AUTHOR'S NOTE

The best friend (besides my husband) God ever gave me is my only sister,
Gail Flowe Purdy. *She has been my Rock, giving encouragement and
sharing wisdom during some of the lowest points in my life. This poem per-
fectly describes our relationship as together we have endured much. It is
written in honor of* ***Gail*** *and all the"* ***true friends"*** *I have had the privilege
of knowing and sharing life with. You know who you are! Thank you for the
love and growth you have allowed me to experience because of having
known you on my journey.*

ANSWERS

I had just been told I had cancer,
Found myself pacing across the floor;
Crying out from the pit of my being,
"Help! I need some *answers*, oh Lord!"

Mastectomy, lumpectomy, to have implants or not,
Is the tram flap procedure best?
From all these choices my brain was boggled,
I needed clarity so my brain could rest.

When in my driveway there drove a florist truck,
And suddenly the doorbell rang;
There stood a woman with a bouquet of flowers, *

143

In my eyes she could see the pain.

I shared with her my story,
Told her I'd just been informed by the doc;
Breast cancer I had, it was in stage one,
And the news my whole world had rocked.

Those flowers were from my dear sister, **
Ordered when she heard my news;
We have such a close relationship,
Her motive was to alleviate my blues.

"Well, I've had the same situation," she said,
"I've journeyed through breast cancer too;"
"I've just been seeking for wisdom," I explained,
"Looks like God is gonna send it through you."

We realized we knew each other,
Hadn't crossed paths in many years;
But she felt my confusion,
Because she had cried the same bitter tears.

Please come inside I encouraged her,
I'd really like to hear more;
I honestly believe that it was God,
Who sent you straight to my door.

She said, "Well I believe it too,
Let me tell you all about it;
I wasn't even supposed to deliver,
So I truly do not doubt it."

My sons are delivering while home from college,
Your arrangement got left behind;
I said, "No problem, of that street I have knowledge,
I'm sure that house I can find."

"So I decided I'd make the delivery,"
At her words I cried even more;
Because this situation we found ourselves in,
Would provide *answers* I was praying for.

Soaking it up as in detail she went,
I listened to her points of view;
In deep conversation, thirty minutes we spent,
Her sister-in-law lived through breast cancer too. ***

I began to feel better as thoughts we shared,
And *answers* gradually came to light;
I had called on the Lord, and he heard my cries,
I knew I wasn't alone in my fight.

We both loved the Lord and it wasn't long,
Before as "sisters" we began praising;
We had things in common and the latest was,
We felt the current situation was amazing.

She lovingly put her arms around me,
I thanked her from the bottom of my heart;
With knowledge she shared and the love she showed,
For making decisions I had a good start.

Much comfort and peace I felt that day,
From all the words she'd been saying;
Then my friend went a little further with it,
From her heart she earnestly began praying.

I kept expressing my gratitude,
As she slowly walked out of the door;
Then after she left, I fell on my knees,
Crying gratefully unto my sweet Lord.

Oh Father, I just want to thank you,

This *journeys* just started I know;
It's true you've never left my side,
You're with me wherever I go.

I've found I can always count on you,
To provide *answers* in my life each day;
I acknowledge it once more, you led her to my door,
And sent a miracle with *answers* my way.

SCRIPTURE REFERENCES
Psalm 18:6, 25:4-6, 118:5, 120:1

———————∞———————

AUTHOR'S NOTE

Dedicated to my breast cancer sisters, ***Joy Jones McClamrock and ***Susie Phillips Jones,** *who provided answers in December 2005 when I was diagnosed and to my physical sister,* ****Gail Flowe Purdy,** *whose caring gift of flowers led to those answers I was seeking.*

———————∞———————

ANTS IN THE SYRUP

"Pass me the syrup," my husband said,
As we ate pancakes at the kitchen table.
His eyesight wasn't very good,
To see without his glasses he wasn't very able.

He generously poured on the syrup,
Over pancakes inside and out.
When I looked down at that sweet covered stack,
I cried out laughing with a shout.

"Oh no, there're *ants in the syrup*,
Why, how in the world can that be?"
They smelled the sweet stuff and found their way up,
To the top of the cabinetry.

The pop top lid was left open,
The ants filed in for a bite.
But much to their surprise,
That sticky stuff would take their life.

They floated around in the syrup,
Like women doing water ballet;
When my husband saw them all over his plate,
Said, "Now what will my breakfast be today?"

I whipped him up a new plateful,
Luckily had another bottle of Log Cabin;
Pancakes and syrup we still frequently have,
But pancakes and ants we're not havin'!

———————— ∞ ————————

BEAGLE ON THE RUN

My husband raises and trains beagles,
They're so cute and cuddly too;
Sweet little pets they are
He's traded, raised, and bought quite a few.

He also hunts rabbits and trains some for that,
Once he borrowed a dog from a friend;
To try out on the next hunting trip,
But that dog escaped from the pen.

To buy it was gonna be more expensive,
Than what he would normally pay;
So when I looked out and saw the dog loose,
I saw dollar signs running away.

I knew if that pup went missing,
And never was to be found;
We'd have to pay for him anyway,
So to catch him I was bound.

Quickly I called a neighbor,
Who came down and nabbed ole "Matt";
He was then put in the kennel
And my thoughts were back on track.

It's funny, and I know it,
But if you do truly know me;
You'd know that I was mostly thinking about,
How I could spend that money at the *Dollar Tree*.

BEAUTY TO BEHOLD

Looked up, saw a beautiful rose bud,
Passed it on my way,
Didn't have time to stop and ponder
It's beauty that certain day.

Went past again days later,
A scent so compelling it shared,
But I had to be at my meeting,
Others were waiting for me there.

Hurried on to my next appointment,
From a distance I could see,
The final progression of that pretty red rose
That had opened so gradually.

Went past the garden weeks later,
And oh, it made me sad,
The sight of that wilted flower
Made my heart sink, made me feel bad.

I wish that I had taken time
It's *beauty to behold,*
It's too late now, it's brown and dead,
The flower has grown old.

My time I should've better controlled,
I missed its fragrance and blended hues;
It was all because of my busy life,
And from having way too much to do.

The petals that once were so elegant,
So symmetrical with overlapping rounds,
To my surprise and to my regret,
Had all fallen down to the ground.

SCRIPTURE REFERENCES
Psalm 19:1, 46:10 ~ Isaiah 40:8 ~ James 4:14

BIRDS AT THE FEEDERS

Bright colored goldfinch
With a robe of sunlit yellow,
I watch you at my feeder
You're such a handsome fella.

Listen to the mockingbird
Those words in song are sung,
Your song imitates other birds perfectly
While it's rolling off your tongue.

All decked out Eastern Flicker
Red streak on the back of your neck,
Like all in the woodpecker family
You retrieve your food with a peck.

Beautiful in flight are you
Mourning dove, mourning dove,
For life, two of you make a pair
As if you are in love.

Look at you sassy jaybird
With blue tail wings and cap,
You make such a noisy call
It lets me know just where you're at.

You have a love for acorns
That drop from the oaks in the fall,
Because of that then, more often you're seen
One of the most decorated birds of all.

Stunning "redbird" cardinal
With black feathers around your orange bill,
You love to forage on the ground

With sunflower seeds you take your fill.

Oh chickadee, sweet chickadee
With your tiny cap of black,
I enjoy seeing you so much
Please keep coming back.

Gorgeous Eastern Bluebird
Recognized for your chestnut brown breast,
You make your home in a nesting box
You're known for bringing happiness.

You are so small little sparrow
Seed eating little creature,
A black line across your face to your eye
Is one of your distinguishing features.

Purple finch, purple finch
Your feathers are dull rose red,
"Why are they called purple?"
I'll never understand.

You create in my fern baskets
A place to call your home,
And when the grands come over
I take them down, your chicks to look upon.

I love to watch you at the suet cakes
Sweet flitty little Carolina Wren,
You carry your tail upright, nest in unusual places
And you have become my friend.

Attractive Red Headed Woodpecker
Digging out wood boring insects,
You light on a tree and I hear your noise:
Rat a tat, tat, peck, peck, peck.

Unusual white breasted nuthatch
You creep down the trees upside down,
With a habit of hiding food in the bark
Going back when there's no one around.

Friendly robin red breast
Your eggs are brilliant blue,
When spring time rolls around
We begin to see much more of you.

Except for the paradise of Hawaii
You make a home in all fifty states.
Could that be because you can not
Make it past the Golden Gate?

Interesting Downy Woodpecker
From the suet blocks, seeds you gather,
As you lean away from the tree you're on
And sit on your tail feathers.

With a small red patch on the back of your head
Why birdwatchers seek you, I understand,
Just like other members of your family
Making beats like a drummer in a band.

Scripture says God sees each sparrow
The very second when from life it falls,
So I know He sees and hears me too
Every time on which Him I call.

SCRIPTURE REFERENCES
Psalm 50:11, Matthew 10:29, 6:25-34, Luke 12:24

Inspired this morning while enjoying the many varieties of birds hovering and perching on my feeders, clinging to the suet baskets and foraging in the grass below. What beauty God has given us to observe and enjoy!

BRAIN FOG

Now why did I even walk in here,
What was I coming to get?
Well, right now I can't think of it,
So let me just go sit a bit.

Oh yes, now I remember,
I need to comb my hair;
Let me go back to my dressing table,
First, gotta get up out of this chair.

I know what I'll do for my memory,
I'll make myself a note;
Uh-oh, now I'm in trouble,
Where's that paper on which I wrote?

Things sometime fail to come back to me,
Now what were my plans for today?
Lord, please help me to keep it all straight,
I sure have a need to pray.

I walk into the kitchen,
Open the cabinet door;
I pick up a box, move a jar,
Oh, what am I looking for?

I cook a lot for the family,
Don't go by many recipes;
Did I put in the salt OR the sugar?
Will my dish be too salty or too sweet?

I need to feed the cats,
The thought to me occurs;
The thought as quickly leaves my brain,
It's brought back when I hear them purrrrr.

It's midday I think I'll meander,
Spend some refreshing time outside;
Oh, wait I've made plans with a neighbor,
But with which one, I can't decide.

I still have my driver's license,
Get in my car and take a nice drive;
When I get to where I'm going,
I wonder if I've arrived.

The seasons pass so quickly,
Is it spring, summer, winter or fall;
What day is this? Let me stop and think,
Some days I can't even recall.

My mind seems to go in circles,
On me, it plays mean tricks;
I try to recall what's my next move,
But the *brain fog* keeps getting thick.

———————— ⌇ ————————

Call Me if You Need Me

Call me if you need me,
My good friend always says,
As we part ways or hang up the phone
I know how much she cares.

She says those same words every time,
Yet, each time they make my heart glad.
It's because from the depths of her heart
I know those words are said.

She's one of the truest friends
That I have ever had.
We've been through a lot together,
We've shared the good and bad.

If there arose a matter
And her help I would need,
I know that she would be there
As many times as those words she's repeated.

Cancer Free

Did he just say the words *"cancer free?"*
Is that what the doctor just now said to me?
Did I just hear him say "no more cancer?"
Thank you dear Jesus my health question is answered!

The pathology report came back all clear,
I'm so thankful it's what I wanted to hear.
Dear Father, you've touched in your loving way,
In response to the unnumbered prayers we've all prayed.

Great mercy you've shown me,
Great grace you've bestowed.
You've carried me through this,
Now you've lightened the load.

To understand why all this happened to me,
Is something on this Earth I may never see.
But God, once more you have faithfully shown,
How much you love me, now my faith has grown.

AUTHOR'S NOTE

This is not to say those who've not received Earthly healing are not loved as much as we who have. God is no respecter of persons (Romans 2:11) and He has plans for each life (Jeremiah 29:11). He loves us all the same (John 3:16) but we must trust in His sovereignty and His omniscience believing that He knows things we do not. (Psalm 33:11, Psalm 139:1-3)

CHANGES TO BE MADE

While looking in the mirror, I see *changes to be made:*
Lint on my clothes, I need a Kleenex for my nose
Stuff on my face, things in the wrong place,
I see *changes to be made,* while looking in my mirror.
Lipstick that is smudgy, my waist a little pudgy,

Here and there an extra pound, has my face ever been so round?
Eyebrows that need waxing, it's all so very taxing!
Hair that needs to be groomed, with youthful looks I'm consumed!
I'm growing old! The world tells me I'm doomed!
The mirror I see before me tells the truth when others lie.
The Bible is like my mirror, God's Word on which I can rely.
While looking in this mirror, God's holy gift to me,
If I'm willing to look closely, I'll see as God sees me.
While looking in this mirror, I see *changes to be made*.....
Sin that needs confessing, salvation that needs professing,
Giving and forgiving to be done, lost souls to be won.
Attitudes need adjusting as holy armor just sits rusting.
I see *changes to be made*.....
Search my heart and know me God, let me not be deceived.
In you I trust, in you I hope, in you I have believed!
Use me Lord, infuse me Lord through the mirror of your Word.
My life you've bought, for my soul you fought, the price for me you
paid.
So your word I'll honor, I'll not be ashamed, I'll be glad to say, I'm
saved!
Then one day when you call me home, my last *change* will be made.
No need for mirrors of any kind when this Earthly flesh I'll trade,
For a new body with life everlasting, no growing old, no sin.
Finally home, my race is run. How thankful I'll be then.
As I enter Heaven's portals, the last *change* I will see.
I'll sing in tune a victory song, your truth has set me free!

AUTHOR'S NOTE

Based on James 1:22-25

CLUBHOUSE

Say, do you want to make a clubhouse?
That's easy, for goodness sake;
A kitchen table, some chairs and a blanket,
Are all the supplies it will take.

Just turn the chairs around backwards,
Move them out from the table a bit;
Throw the blanket on top of them all,
Oh, think of the fun of it!

Good times can be had in a clubhouse,
Hiding from bad guys outside;
Pretending to be on a spaceship,
Or perhaps a magic carpet ride.

Playing cops and robbers,
Setting up a stake out in the dark;
Pretending to be pirates,
On a voyage about to embark.

Playing Army, safari, or hiding from a monster,
Imagination is the key;
Let children have fun in a clubhouse,
Only one time a child they will be.

If the children get restless or weary,
Or need to pass time on a rainy day;
Just provide some fun like I do,
Build a *clubhouse* in which they can play.

COUGHING SPELL

Good grief, I'm having a coughing spell,
I've taken all I can stand.
Somebody give me a cough drop please,
Put it right here in my hand.

I'll put it in my mouth so fast,
Oh yes, and I'll decree:
That when after a while in my mouth it's been,
My coughing spell has eased.

———————⟳———————

COUPON QUEEN

Years ago when things were lean,
My family nicknamed me the *"Coupon Queen"*.
I carried a stack, found them everywhere I'd look,
Gathered them from magazines, newspapers, and books.
They'd sure come in handy.
I'd save pennies, nickels, dimes.
Now I can save dollars
Especially at double dip times.

I collect them for restaurants,
The grill, the cafe, the deli.
It's good to save a dollar
As I go to fill my belly.
I save on groceries, at retail stores,
and super-duper markets,
Places like K-mart and Walmart,

Places like Bi-Lo and Target.

I'd like to know the total
Of the money I've saved through the years
By just using my common sense and a pair of kitchen shears.
So if you go somewhere with me
Don't let it be a surprise
If I pull out a coupon
That saves on your food and mine.

It's for sure if I needed a coupon
To enter Heaven's door,
Oh, I'd be out there looking,
I bet I'd find one for sure.
But the greatest of blessings
That a blessing could be
Is that Jesus paid my way and yours
and that it's absolutely free!

SCRIPTURE REFERENCES
Matthew 20:28 ~ Romans 6:23 ~ I Corinthians 6:19-20 ~ Revelation 5:9

DAUGHTER IN LOVE

Not born of my body,
Not blood of my blood,
Not raised in my household,
But loved with my love.

The daughter I always dreamed of,
The daughter I never knew,

God gifted me with the next best thing,
And our bond as in-laws grew.

Joined in marriage to my baby boy,
She has brought to my life an abundance of joy,
She cooks, she cleans, she stays constantly in motion,
For family, friends, and faith she has such strong devotion.

Beautiful, caring, and kind is she,
As much like a daughter as a girl could be,
Always checking in, always showing up,
A confidante, a true friend, never void of love.

My precious God given daughter-in-law,
With her unselfish, good natured ways,
Brings light to every corner,
That her heart of gold conveys.

With her genuine kind-hearted actions,
Truly sent from Heaven above,
She's not only my daughter-in-law,
She's also my *daughter-in-love!*

SCRIPTURE REFERENCES
Ruth 1:16-17

AUTHOR'S NOTE

I'm thankful for the two "daughters-in-love" God has blessed me with. They (***Jeanne and Tara***) *are so precious and are the inspiration for this poem.*

DIPPIN'

It was summer in the 60's,
On grandma's concrete porch.
In the evenings we'd catch lightning bugs,
We loved to watch their torch.

In the daytime we'd get thirsty,
But instead of merely sippin',
We'd get some liquid in a cup,
Act like grandma and pretend to be *dippin'.*

We'd get one of grandma's colored cups,
And play as if we were spittin'.
Sometimes we'd be rockin' on the glider,
Sometimes on the front steps sittin'.

We'd press our lips with our fingers
And get a steady aim.
Water, Kool-Aid, tea, snuff substitutes,
As we'd spew from our mouths unashamed.

We'd laugh and whoop and holler.
We'd giggle and frolic and play.
Such enjoyment we were finding,
In the simplicity of those childhood days.

DIRT THERAPY

When I feel the need for therapy,
It's out to my garden I go.
It sure eases my tension, puts my mind in suspension,
I love to plant and watch things grow.

As I play in the dirt my mind wanders,
Takes me back in time as a child.
Then it moves me to planning day after day,
And the things I must do in a while.

Weeds they need a pullin',
Bulbs planted, seeds wait to be sown.
When I get lost in my garden,
That time brings sweet peace to my soul.

In springtime the works of my labor,
Begin to grow and sprout.
The stalks show themselves like peeping Toms,
And the leaves begin to come out.

Next the tiny buds begin forming,
As I enter the garden I see,
I've got to be there, in good fresh air,
'Cause this time is like therapy for me.

The bright sun keeps on bringing,
It's beautiful, warm, golden rays.
The flowers pop out in their glory,
And their various colors display.

I pick a fresh bouquet of jonquils,
Them to a neighbor I take.
The smile on her face, nothing else could replace,
She no longer can dig, hoe, or rake.

As neighbors walk by they tell me,
How much they enjoy the view.
They see me working all the time,
I could use a whole garden crew.

So this time consuming hobby,
Is not only good for me;
It brings joy to many others,
While serving as my therapy.

EGGS

I like them scrambled,
I like them boiled,
I like them sunny side up.
I like them over easy,
Great grandma drinks them raw from a cup!

Use them in a cake,
In sweet cookies bake,
They're fun to dye at Easter time.
Mix them up in a breakfast casserole,
That use is a favorite of mine.

What a versatile food item
Those delicious *eggs* truly are!

Some people throw them at bad concerts,
At Halloween they get thrown at cars.

When *eggs* are around a healthy meal can be made,
Crack the shells brown or white,
There's protein in every size and grade.
Serve 'em up however you like

Omelets are usually well liked too...
With a combo of cheese, onions, and bacon,
Peppers, mushrooms, sour cream can be used.
Some buffets have omelets for the takin'.

They're great at reunions and parties,
Deviled and served on a pretty plate.
I bet you'd be surprised to hear
Of the number of eggs I have ate!
(Yes, I know it should be *have eaten* but that doesn't rhyme.)

Eggs can create a rich conditioner
For your hair following a shampooing.
Rinse with cold water after a few minutes,
Not hot water or cooked *eggs* you'll be brewing.

Whip them up high with a mixer,
Make fluffy meringue for a pie.
If they shake inside when you pick them up,
Better let those rotten *eggs* lie!

Oh hear me as I share with you
This one final thought I beg.
It's really pretty amazing, don't you think,
God formed us all from an *egg*?!

EMOTIONS

Emotions, we all have them.
Man, they can drive you nuts!
They can cause you just like a roller coaster ride
To spew and spill your guts.

They come in all forms and fashions
Bringing happiness, grief, or fear.
They stick with you forever.
They start out as baby tears.

When you are messed up, mixed up, or bothered
Upset and bent out of shape,
Emotions are the culprit,
Control of your mind they take.

Rulers of your thought processing,
Telling you what you want, think, and feel.
They'll get you all excited,
And then they'll break the deal.

Your mind can be changed in a minute,
Going from good to bad.
Emotions are sure to make you have
The strongest feelings you've ever had.

You can switch from crying to laughing
or vice versa 'cause they don't care.
Emotions are quick, with a heartbeat they change,
Before you become aware.

So watch them and realize their power,
God gave them to you so they're good.
He gave them to you for a purpose -

To guard and control them you should.

It's difficult, I know, but you can trust me.
The gamut of *emotions* I've felt.
Sorrow, pain, fear, endless heartbreak,
Laughter, joy and peace, life has dealt.

Because we're all human we experience
That coaster of *emotions* we ride.
And because we're all human we need help too,
With controlling those feelings inside.

The Bible tells us when we follow Jesus
As Lord and Savior of our soul,
The precious Holy Spirit then enters,
To be the one to take control.

At the very minute of salvation,
He enters through that open door...
The one you've kept locked so tightly,
Never wanting to open before.

At the moment you receive Him,
He makes himself a home inside.
Only if you let Him,
Will He take away your pride.

The hurt, the fear, the self-centeredness,
All those ungodly flings,
When He makes your heart's door His entrance,
And exchanges those for much better things.

It's a day by day long process.
It doesn't happen overnight.
And only if you allow His power,
Can He change your thinker to think right.

Emotions, we all have them.
Decide who you'll let be in charge.
They can make you feel weak,
Make you strong when you speak,
Or through life like a raging bull barge.

We can seek to do good to others,
Realizing they too have known pain,
Or let our *emotions* run ragged,
But really, how much would we gain?

It's hard to think first of others
When our problems so overwhelm.
It's easier when you know Jesus,
With the sweet Holy Spirit at the helm.

Lord, you gave me these *emotions:*
I'm hurt, I'm mad, it's not right!
OK Lord, you help me handle it,
'Cause you know how I want to shine bright!

ENJOY THE LITTLE THINGS

Learn to *enjoy the little things*
That happen along the way.
Learn to see the little things
In your life day by day.

Simple acts of kindness,
Done for you once in a while.
When a stranger on the street

Gives a nod or a friendly smile.

Sweet surprises of nature,
God will let you see.
Learn to look out for them,
A little happiness they may bring.

Looking up in the evening
To see cotton candy colored skies.
Sharing a belly laugh
Till tears roll from your eyes.

Breakfast in bed...
Coloring in red...
Compliments said...
Getting photo creds....

Adding salt and pepper
To your personal taste.
Making crafts with children
Of what normally would be waste.

The fragrant smell of an orange
When you peel off its skin.
The feel of hearing your favorite song
When its first notes begin.

A lone yellow daffodil,
Blooming out in the woods.
Doing for yourself hard things
You never thought you could.

A caring friend's text
Asking how you're doing today.
A young child approaching
Asking you to stop and play.

An encouraging word,
A light pat on the back,
Your family lets you
Stay later in the sack.

Feeling the warm summer sunshine,
As it hits your face.
Going shopping at the mall,
Finding a close parking place.

A chocolate chip cookie
Or other tasty things.
Grandma's raw cake batter
Or a plate of barbecued wings.

Looking at a tiny ant
Through a magnifying glass.
When you're at the checkout line,
And a nice person lets you pass.

When the date is over and done,
Steal a kiss in the pale moonlight.
Then you look into each other's eyes,
And you know everything's alright.

The soft winds as they create,
Tunes through the swaying wind chimes.
Learn to enjoy all kinds of little things,
And all sorts of simple times.

How about a friendly bear hug?
Wanna dig in the dirt for doodlebugs?
Have a good cup of coffee in your favorite mug.
Hey look, there's a polka dotted ladybug!

If little things don't get your attention,
If you, they never amaze,
Then ask God for a change of heart -
Let him brighten and change your ways.

SCRIPTURE REFERENCES
Ecclesiastes 3:12-13, 5:19, 6:9, 7:14, 8:15 ~ John 16:33

EYE EXAM

Hey there, eye doctor,
Tell me what you know.
I'm here to check my vision
And to see what the exam will show.

Things are getting kind of blurry
And a tad bit out of focus.
Tell me what you see,
What I'm seeing is just bogus.

I'm calling out the letters
T S U R and V.
The bottom line is sketchy,
Looks like C F O and Z.

Put some drops into my eye
For quick pupil dilation.
Diagnose any sort of disease,
Aid in checking my medical condition.

With a wisp of air,
Check the pressure in my eye.

When that little test is over,
My eyeballs breathe a sigh.

"Look straight ahead," you instruct me,
As you shine the bright light in my face.
Then with my eyes you tell me
Your finger's movement to trace.

From your line of vision you see
retina, lens, and amazing optic nerve.
It's the only part of the central nervous system
Doctors can easily observe.

It is uniquely a part of both the eye and brain.
They constantly send messages to each other.
Of distance, details and direction,
Accomplishing much as they look out for one another.

Glaucoma, macular degeneration,
Retinal detachment, and cataract:
Take a good look now doctor,
Because those, my healthy vision will impact.

I'm glad I have you doctor,
When floaters in my eyes I see.
Or other aggravating issues
Like pink eye or redness from allergies.

Look at all the facts
Then write a corrective prescription.
I already know I need new glasses,
It's hard to give any good descriptions.

Go back to work, sit at my desk,
Can't read, sorta hard to even write.
It's all because my dilated pupils

Are letting in way too much light!

SCRIPTURE REFERENCES
Psalm 119:37 ~ Proverbs 20:12 ~ Matthew 6:22-23 ~ 1 Corinthians 2:9
Hebrews 12:2

FIREFLIES

Tiny blinking lights cross the sky
Taking charge of the night;
It's not a bunch of UFOs
It's a bunch of *fireflies.*

Off and on their gold lights blink
Like caution traffic signals;
Catch and put them in a jar
Watch "lightning bugs" bring awe and giggles.

They land on the trees and shrubbery too
Members of the beetle clan;
Making use of bioluminescence
Catch them, gently hold them in your hand.

Throw them high into the sky
And watch as they take their flight;
Strange little creatures they are for sure
Amazing glow worms called *fireflies.*

FLOWER POWER

In winter, I look out my window
I see grays, blacks, browns and greens;
Months later, from the same window
I view colors so beautiful to me.

God in his miraculous power
Brings from the gloom and drear,
Sights glorious and oh so breathtaking
My flowers as they bloom each year.

Bulbs buried deep in the darkness
From the coldness of winter they rise;
Pitch blackness cannot hold them
Like birthdays they bring their surprise.

Unfolding with reds, yellows, purples,
Pinks, oranges, fuschias and blues,
The colors so grand and enchanting
Like a seasoned artist would choose.

Yes, springtime in all of its glory
Comes about for His power to show;
Have you ever thought about it...
There is a master artist you know?

Its wonder and long awaited arrival,
Its palette of beautiful hues,
Are just another soft reminder;
So let the *flower power*
Speak His power to you.

SCRIPTURE REFERENCES

Genesis 1:1 ~ Jeremiah 32:17 ~ John 1:3 ~ Romans 1:20 ~ Colossians 1:16
Revelation 4:11

———— ✧ ————

FLY IN A COMA

It's summertime and I'm so thirsty
I need a drink of water.
I go to my refrigerator
'Cause it couldn't get much hotter!
I spy a black spot on the bowl
Containing chocolate pudding.
I pick it up and realize
It's a fly and oh no, He shouldn't -
Have flown into my refrigerator
Oh, what's he doing there?
Use your head! It's hot outside!
He came to cool off in despair!
Well, he made the mistake of a lifetime,
A better choice should be -
'Cause a cold refrigerator
Does damage to the likes of he.
He could fly no longer
The frostbite got him down.
I looked in his eyes and feared for his life,
No hope for him was found.
I guess the temptation overtook him,
Was it the coolness or the aroma?
Believe it or not, the shock of it all
Had put that *fly in a coma!*

———— ✧ ————

GLITTER TRAIL

I bought a new dress oh, so pretty,
Of black velvet so soft it was made.
Adorned with silver glitter in swirly patterns,
When I saw it to buy it I was bade.

Look closely you'll know why I like it,
It sparkles and glistens you see.
If ever I get lost and have that dress on,
You could very easily find me.

Only one time a year do I wear it,
But one time is enough I can tell.
Cause it constantly drops its glitter,
And everywhere I've been there's a trail!

GOD'S SURPRISES

God's surprises are everywhere,
Just open your eyes and you'll see them there;
A gray squirrel darting across the street,
A beautiful sunrise at the beach.

Take a walk deep in the woods,
Find a speckled newborn fawn;
Momma's hid him nestled in the shadows,
Camouflaged but she's still looking on.

Hiking on the nature trail,
Been there about an hour;
Stop for a break, look across the way,
See a patch of purple wildflowers.

Green moss, to one's feet feels like carpet,
So God's carpet it must be;
Look higher, overhead and listen,
To the talented mockingbird sing.

While fishing at the lake house,
Red and white bobber hits the water with a plop;
Suddenly hear a shuffling noise,
It's a blue heron, he just landed on the dock.

Walking into the grocery store,
Need a quarter for the cart;
Look down, surprise it's just what you need,
A shiny quarter in the parking lot!

God's surprises can elevate you
If you're a little down inside;
He seeks to brighten up your day,
So little surprises He will provide.

You might miss them if you're not looking,
You won't see them as surprises if you don't choose;
If you've never thought about little things this way,
I hope this poem will change your point of view.

GOOSE ATTACK

I parked in the lot at Party City,
Thinking matching tableware would make things look pretty.
When there in the grass across the way,
A couple of geese in the median lay.
Oh they looked so peaceful
As I glanced in their direction,
But when I started toward the store
I realized I needed protection.
One of the geese ran toward me
Hissing with wings spread high.
Dear God! I must have upset it!
Is it preparing to fly?
All I did was get out of my car
And proceed to go inside,
So what's got this goose all fired up,
Something has definitely turned the tide.
Oh no! It's not flying,
It's waddling straight my way.
There's no place to hide and nowhere to run,
Something tells me it doesn't want to play.
I've never seen a goose get mean,
OK, now I see the reason.....
Another goose follows close behind,
I bet it's mating season.
Do I look like a threat to him?
Why, I wouldn't even dare,
To take a chance at separating
Such a lovely pair.
Well, it's too late, he thinks so;
Good grief, he's about to explode.
The only defense I have here
Is a big pocketbook that's loaded.
My mind races as he comes closer;

Oh boy, it's for real, he's attacking!
And just what am I supposed to do?
Of all times, I have no backing.
I'll take your head off with this purse!
Seems it would be justified,
'Cause at this point the way you look
It could be your life for mine!
I flail and fling and shout out loud:
"Get away, you silly goose!
You'd better back off big boy
'Cause this pocketbook is loose!
I'll use it like a missile,
I'll send your hide a flyin',
And when I tell this story
Friends will think that I am lyin'."
It's true, for sure it happened
In the parking lot that day,
I won the battle, I scared him off,
and then proudly went on my way.

AUTHOR'S NOTE

True story...I think the geese were actually just protecting their nest. Of course, like we all do, I looked around to see if anyone was watching that escapade!

HAVE A WONDERFUL DAY!

Our conversation ended with these words:
"Have a wonderful day!"
They brightened up my morning,
And encouraged me on my way.

If you know of someone who needs them,
One who needs a little lift,
Just phone them or speak as you walk by,
As through your mind these words drift.

A stranger, a friend, a companion,
We all need the smile these words bring.
They can change a heart that is breaking,
Into one that is yearning to sing.

Speak words of blessings along life's path,
So many are discouraged and blue.
They long to hear a good word,
And that word can come from you.

So look for them, they're everywhere,
To their spirit these words could say:
"Even though times are troubling and cares are great,
It's alright, God's still good, it's OK."

SCRIPTURE REFERENCES
Proverbs 12:25 ~ Galatians 6:2 ~ Ephesians 4:29

180

HE'S SNORING ZZZZZ

He's snoring like a freight train
Rolling on the tracks.
When my husband snores way,
I roll him on his back.

He'll breathe kinda light for a little while,
And then he starts again,
Snoring like a freight train
Rolling around the bend.

I'm tempted to kick him outta the bed,
If I didn't love him like no other.
I'd also contemplate the idea
Of him, with a pillow to smother.
(All in fun and for rhyming purposes only; no true intentions are
implied!!)

Zzzzzzzzzzzzz Zzzzzzzzzzzzz
ZZZZZZZZZZZZZZZZZZZZZZ
ZZZZZZZZZzzzzzzzzzzzz
ZZZZZZZZZZZZZZZZZZZZZZ!!!!

HEAR THEIR SONG

While walking out to the old potting shed,
I heard the birds singing over my head.
At first, I didn't hear their song,
But then to their happy tunes, I was drawn.

The reason my heart their glee did not share,
I was thinking lots of things while going out there.

It's for sure today held much to do,
Because of that, I was on a mission;
Feed the cats, cut the grass,
Clean up that messy kitchen.
Pick up some groceries, pay some bills,
Had an appointment with my physician.

But all of the sudden,
I came to my senses,
Of my surroundings became more aware.
Oh the beauty I'd have been missing,
If I hadn't have taken a listen,
To the flocks and the fowls of the air.

SCRIPTURE REFERENCES
Psalm 104:12 ~ Matthew 6:26

Hot Flash

I'm burning up and I'm on fire,
To cool my body is my desire.
Can't take this heat there's a *hot flash* coming on.
I'm entering in the "old age" zone.

Sweat drops keep forming on my body,
Oh goodness right now, it's true I'm "a hottie".
My hair is clinging to the back of my neck,
I think I need a radiator check!

My face is red and my palms are moist,
When this is over, I'm going to rejoice!
Here's my money, doc it's all **COLD** cash,
Help me, please help me. I'm having a ***HOT*** *flash!!*

IN STYLE

Is it *in style*? Is it not?
It doesn't matter so much to me.
If I like it, I'll wear it,
If I don't, then I won't,
If I'm not sure...
Well then, we'll just see.

INSOMNIA

My goodness, I can't go to sleep,
Everything's buzzing in my head;
I should've just stayed up all night,
Why did I even get in bed?

My man is constantly snoring,
For the noise I can't even think straight;
I try to get my mind off stuff,
Lordy, it's getting sooo late!

I look at the clock and it's midnight,
Why soon, it'll be time to get up;
His snoring reminds me of a freight train,
That from the tracks is about to jump.

Plans and promises and particulars,
Keep dancing in my brain;
I wish I could just turn them off,
Oh my goodness, what a pain!

Finally feel myself getting sleepy,
Thank goodness for that fact;
Then the clock goes off, it's time to get up,
But I feel like I've just hit the sack!

It's All in Fun

When all the gang gets together,
We kid and we prod and we poke;
Say crazy things to each other,
Are they the truth? Shucks, no!

Oh, *it's all in fun*, believe me,
No need to get upset;
Every time the gang gets together,
On shenanigans you can bet!

As we laugh at each other and banter,
We each gently criticize;
Everyone knows *it's all in fun*,
You can tell by the look in our eyes.

It never gets to be too much,
Sometimes we turn red with laughter;
Everyone knows it's gonna be their turn,
'Cause it's only a good chuckle we're after!

When the time comes to leave each other,
No feelings are hurt by the jokes;
No egos are damaged, no harm has been done,
By the foolishness we've all just spoke.

So we shake hands or hug at our leaving,
Our friend time is over and done;
We go on our way with a smile in our hearts,
Knowing it's all good, cause *it's all in fun!*

IT'S RAINING

Look outside, *it's raining!*
Grab my umbrella and run.
Gotta go to work today,
Sure wish I could see the sun!

Look now, it's still raining!
Time to leave, going out to my car.
The winds are so gusty, the trees are waving,
Oh, umbrella, don't know where you are!

Look outside, *it's raining!*
All the chores are done.
The grands are here, and we don't care,
Rain dancing and puddle jumping for fun!

Look outside, *it's raining!*
And it's a "gully washer".
The ditches are full, the pond overflows,
Better slip on those galoshes.

AUTHOR'S NOTE

*Dedicated to my oldest son, **Keith**, who as a very young child, drew a beautiful watercolor of a little boy with his rain suit, galoshes, and umbrella as a classroom assignment. I've always loved the simplicity of it and the pale colors he chose. His childhood drawing, which has been something this Mom could never part with, has served as the inspiration for "It's Raining."*

KEEP A LID ON IT

Express yourself, confess yourself,
Don't need to be a doormat;
But look inside, drop some pride,
And leave SOME things where they're at.

God will give you wisdom,
He'll take good care of you;
If you can get strength to hold your peace,
There're things he'll point out too.

Do you want to go back to the pain of the past,
To gut punched feelings that you can't outcast?
Do you want to go back to detective ways,
To broken thoughts and hard earned days?

When the memories and the hurt have settled
To the bottom of your heart,
You've let sleeping dogs lie and forgiveness reign;
Don't give trouble and unrest a new start.

Say what you feel is right,
But don't add evil to the spice of life;
Yes, Satan stirs the pot once we open the lid,
Relationships and good times can suddenly take a skid.

Everything's right with friends and family,
So just keep that happy going;
Don't spoil it all with an attitude,
Or gossip seeds that you might be sowing.

Nobody gets their way all the time,
If they do, their day is coming;
Nobody's opinion is right all the time,
If they think that, their brain is numbing.

I've thought to myself I know better,
"Ewww, why'd I say that? Doggone it!"
I've learned to be wise, keep it to myself,
And to put it simply..."Keep a lid on it"!

SCRIPTURE REFERENCES
Proverbs 4:23-24, 12:18, 18:21, 16:18 ~ Mark 3:24-25
Philippians 3:12-14 ~ James 1:5

LET'S BUILD A SNOWMAN

Come on, let's build a snowman,
We'll give him a carrot nose.
Pat out a snowball, roll it around on the ground,
Make three sizes and stacked up they'll go.

Raid Momma's well stocked sewing basket,
Find two black buttons for his eyes.
Put three more down the front of his pretend jacket,
How he ends up looking will be a surprise.

Need to find him the perfect topper,
What kind of hat should we use?
Well, I say he's our snowman -
We can use any hat that we choose.

Tie a red bandana around his neck,
Or a scarf to bring color to his life.
Put Daddy's belt around his waist,
Might not fit, might be way too tight.

Find just the right sticks to make his two arms,
Ones that also, seem to have fingers.
Go back to Momma's basket and find red yarn,
For a big happy smile that lingers.

Just use your imagination,
For snowmen there are no rules.
Everyone who passes will stare and say:
"Jeepers, that snowman is cool!"

Stand back, admire your creation,
With all the neighborhood kids.
To build a snowman together,
Is one of the most fun things we ever did.

LOVE YA, LOVE YA, LOVE YA

"Love ya, love ya, love ya,"
With a hug and those last words we part.
They walk out the door,
Get into the car,
And away down the road goes my heart!

MAKE A CHILD FEEL LOVED

All it takes is a little time
To *make a child feel loved.*
A story read, a piggy back ride,
A long walk or a real tight hug.

Sometimes it calls for putting aside
Things that at the time seem so vital.
Things that really aren't that important,
Things that in the long run are trifle.

Replace those with making memories,
Get out paper, markers, and glue.

Look in the cabinets for pots and pans,
Cut up veggies and make a stew.

Dress up in a silly costume,
Run wildly around in the yard.
Play a game of tag or chase,
Catch bugs and put them in a jar.

Hide and Seek, Hungry Hippo,
Spend an hour in the sandbox.
Pitch the ball, comb their "bed head" hair,
Wow, talk about dreadlocks!

Broaden their horizons,
Take them to the zoo.
Get out the funny red nose,
Put on some big clown shoes.

Sit down and explain the Bible,
Upon illustrations of its heroes look.
Get out the bright colored crayons,
Get out some fun coloring books.

All it takes is a little time,
Children don't really care what you do.
You'd be surprised how just a few moments,
Can say to a child, "I love you!"

SCRIPTURE REFERENCES
Psalm 127:3-5 ~ Proverbs 17:6, 22:6 ~ Mark 10:13-16 ~ Ephesians 6:4

———————— ∞ ————————

MAKE A PROJECT

"Mimi, can we *make a project?*"
That's the question they always ask.
When my grandchildren come over,
I'm always up to the task.

Get out the crayons and markers,
Put newspaper on the table.
They love to *"make a project,"*
Doing the best that they are able.

Get well cards and greetings
Of construction paper and cut outs,
Such talent this Mimi has never seen,
Those grands are mine, there's no doubt!

Creating a pretty fleece blanket,
Tying the cut sections in knots.
Use a pattern with sweet cat faces,
'Cause lots of cats we've got.

Making cupcakes, painting ornaments,
Or lollipops to share with all.
When it's project time at Mimi's,
Every one of us has a ball!

When we're done there's a big mess to clean up,
Glue, paint, batter, or flour everywhere.
But the love and the laughs and the memories,
I hope forever we'll share.

The mess it makes in my kitchen and den,
With the fun we have doesn't compare.
This Mimi loves her grandbabies,
Wants them to forever remember my care!

AUTHOR'S NOTE

*In honor of my four precious grandchildren, (**Fisher, Carson, Raelyn and Barrett**) who are now much older, but no less loved.*

MAKE UP'S MAGIC DOOR

I get up and put on makeup,
And oh the changes I see.
When I get out my bag of tricks,
It makes a different woman of me.

If I'm feeling sick or in a bad mood,
I get busy and "fix" my face.
I have two drawers full of makeup,
The wrinkles of time they erase.

Mascara, eye shadow, concealer,
All these sure come in good.
The makeup base my flaws erase,
And help me look better than I normally would.

At my house, there is a *magic door,*
For a while it's been given that name.
Cause when Momma goes in and she finally walks out,
She never looks the same!

MOVIE DAY

Can't tell you all the movies
That we have gone to see.
Tuesdays in the summer was *movie day*
For the four grandchildren and me.

We'd give the ticket clerk our dollars
And hurriedly rush on in.
To get a good seat just in time,
This Mimi felt like a Momma hen.

What warmed my heart so much about it
Was how the grands always had big smiles.
We'd check out the restroom, grab our snacks,
Then we'd head on down the aisle.

Yum! Buttery popcorn and candy,
Everyone also got a soft drink.
We'd find our place and get settled,
As into the comfortable seats we'd sink.

Each of us looked forward to *movie day,*
Delightful smells wafted in the air.
And as the lights turned way down low,
We sat there without a care.

All got quiet as the curtain pulled back,
"Shhh!! The movie is about to start!"
Lord, let those days be remembered by them,
With fondness, let those days fill their hearts.

AUTHOR'S NOTE

*When my four grands (**Fisher, Carson, Raelyn and Barrett**) were young, Tuesday was dollar day at the local movie theater. Snacks were priced low and most families could enjoy the inexpensive weekly treat. This poem was inspired by the numerous trips we made to the theater and by the love and laughter we shared each week during those fun summer "movie days".*

MR. TURKEY

Oh, *Mr. Turkey,*
How you doin'?
Oh, I be doin' fine.
But when November rolls around,
I think I'll run and hide!

MY ATTIC

There's all sorts of things in *my attic,*
Things given, collected, and inherited;
When seasons change, I change things too,
So to go to *my attic* is imperative!

I climb the stairs to get up there,
It's organized disaster;
For Valentines, Easter, St. Patrick's through fall.
There's much to decorate with–I have it all!

Come Christmas, I drag down the wreaths and the boxes,
My husband says from things, I need detoxin';
He says if one more thing in *my attic* goes,
Our ceiling will come falling down -
Well it just might…..who knows?

The kids, grands, and friends all call me to ask,
If in *my attic* I have what they need;
Well I probably do, you know me,
Give me a minute, I'll climb up and see.

I bring stuff down, and I put stuff back,
It's a bunch of stuff–there's not much I lack;
Its lots of junk, to me lots of treasure,
The attachment I have cannot be measured.

I decorate my house, my church, and my yard,
I plan fun parties and dinners;
To practice hospitality, sharing, and caring,
I can't be considered a beginner.

A friend, years ago wrote a poem about me,
Her lyrics went this way:

"When Shirley enters the Pearly Gates,
She'll ask if they need matching napkins, cups, and plates."

Yes, I know there is lots of stuff up there,
My husband says, "Give some of that away."
I say, "Oh no, I can't do that,
Someone else might need it someday."

He jokingly says after my time has passed,
Soon after my days are spent,
He'll gather it up and to haul it away,
A big dump truck he's going to rent.

I say, "Oh please, now honey,
You know you can't do that;
There's too much good stuff to destroy it all,
What if you marry another pack rat?"

It'll come in handy again someday
When you find someone else to marry;
She might just enjoy *my attic* stuff too,
And you certainly know how to carry!

Though, for now, it's upstairs if it's needed,
I go carefully, 'cause I'm past my prime;
But the enjoyment the stuff brings,
And the blessings through it I share,
Bring a smile to me as I climb.

My Bible, My Dear Old Friend

Many years ago a Bible I purchased,
This would be one for myself.
I read it consistently, carried it proudly,
It was never just left on a shelf.

It's cover of sturdy maroon leather,
With words of Jesus in red,
From trusting in the promises of its chapters,
I've been plagued with less fear and dread.

I've found in its words great comfort,
Through inspiration from God it was written.
As I read its pages, I've sensed His presence,
By His unconditional love I've been smitten.

Through the years of study and reading,
My Bible gradually became so worn.
Once I traveled from church with it atop my car,
When I recovered it, lots of pages were torn.

Yes, its pages are tattered, book markers all scattered,
Its margins with highlighted notes are filled.
When the words come to life and jump off of the page,
I start feeling those Holy Ghost chills.

In a zip up cover I placed it,
To keep it from falling apart;
Sure I know I could buy a new Bible,
But this Bible knows me by heart.

Yellow tear stains can be detected,
As the pages are one by one turned.

Tears came from a heart of heaviness,
Or as for repentance and obedience I yearned.

Tears that came from feeling a great sense of peace,
From the feeling of His compassionate touch;
From finding joy in His presence,
Understanding more deeply His love.

A lot I've gained from its stories,
Of parables and characters of all sorts;
Its helped me to stay on track in life,
When my mission Satan sought to abort.

So even though it looks like
A book a stray dog has chewed on,
I'm not so proud that I won't say
In much time, through it I have grown.

It's been sent away for rebinding,
Before it's too late and it sees its end;
When I'm dead and gone let my children be reminded,
It was *my Bible, my dear old friend.*

SCRIPTURE REFERENCES
Joshua 1:8 ~ Psalm 119:105 ~ Isaiah 40:8, 55:11 ~ Matthew 4:4, 7:24,
24:35 ~ Romans 1:16, 10:17, 15:4 ~ II Timothy 3:16-17 ~ Hebrews 4:12-14

MY PERSONAL ELMER FUDD

My husband is a wabbit (rabbit) hunter
There's not much that he loves more,
Than to hunt with friends and family
Oh, there's hunting stories galore!

He puts on his orange "you see me" hat
And his winter warm camouflage clothes,
How many rabbits will the dogs stir up?
It's anyone's guess, who knows?

The guys all pile into the hunting truck
Their excitement, oh how it shows,
As in that multi-colored Suburban
My husband and his good buddies go!

He comes home tired and worn out
From hill climbing, briar stomping, and walking.
Were the dogs on it today? How'd they do?
Did they do a good job of stalking?

Good day or bad, I welcome him home,
He's my best friend, my pal, my bud.
I love to see him enjoying life,
He's *my personal Elmer Fudd!*

AUTHOR'S NOTE

In honor of my husband, **Mitchell,** *who has since I've known him had a passion for his beagles and a good rabbit hunt.*

MY VOTE

A man who loves our country,
A woman who leads with wisdom,
A candidate who truly serves the people
And to the peoples' voices they listen.

Apple pie, peach, or cherry,
Vanilla or chocolate ice cream,
Just give me the ooiest, gooiest kind -
Nothing plain for me.

Chinese, American, Italian, or Mexican,
I'm not picky about my cuisine.
I'll let you choose where we eat tonight -
No *vote*, they all sound good to me.

I text, I call, I email too,
But none of these gets my *vote*.
Like a long summer visit on the front porch swing
Or a sincere handwritten note.

Let's make our plans and get it on the schedule,
Where are we going for vacation?
To the mountains, the beach, or a Caribbean Isle?
My vote is for the most exciting destination!

The ballgame, a movie, friends' game night -
Just what would you like to do?
I don't really care so you decide -
My vote is to just be with you.

NEW SHOES

Girl, do you want to go shopping?
I want to get some new *shoes*.
You know what, I don't really need any,
But I'd still like to go with you.

Although we both have a closet full,
Let's go! Let's head to the store.
Come on then, you know you can't stand it,
I know you'll end up buying more.

Just bought a new dress for the formal,
I need the perfect *shoes* to match.
So I thought you'd like to ride along,
Bet we'll come home with a big ole batch.

Now, we're looking over the selection,
So many great choices there are.
Sandals, wedges, flat bottoms and boots -
We might need help getting them to the car.

Let's try on these fun chukkas,
We find so many *shoes* we like.
Some are so cute and some are so comfy,
Must we even consider the price?

Don't you just love trying on all these -
Mary Jane's, clogs, and high heels?
I value your opinion, but, like them or not,
I've got to have these cute espadrilles!

Look at these, I really don't need them,
But I'd like to have something new.
Tell me what do you think of this style,

They're such adorable, flat bottomed *shoes*.

Think I'll get these good fitting sneakers,
They'll be great for jogging in the park.
They've even got those reflective bands
That will shine if I'm running when it's dark.

Oh, I really love these stilettos,
With these on, attention I'd gain.
But do I even want that attention,
If that attention is gonna cause my feet pain?

Oh goodness, I'm over here cracking up,
Seeing you in those combat boots.
You always make shopping so much fun,
Girlfriend, you are such a hoot!

Can't believe that I'm saying this,
I'm worn out from all this trying on.
Next time, we'll have to come back here,
But for now, we need to get gone!

We each find our cards and pay at the counter,
Then we finally start to leave the store.
When set up right there is another display,
And we both find ourselves wanting more.

Let me count how many pairs I just purchased,
Well I don't even have a clue.
But like me, most women will assuredly say:
"A girl can never have too many *shoes!*"

ODE TO ELVIS

In the winter of '77,
I received a special call.
This question then was asked of me
By my favorite sister-in-law.*

"Do you want to see *ELVIS* in concert?
The tickets are going on sale."
"For real, you have to ask me???
On that offer you know I won't bail!!!"

I'm like so many others,
Been lovin' him since I was young.
Most all his movies I have seen,
Most all his songs I've sung.

So we got our golden tickets,
Drove to the Charlotte Coliseum.
Along with a building full of fans
Who just couldn't wait to see him.

One could feel the level of excitement
Growing stronger in the room.
When the music started and the house lights dimmed,
Our hearts were racing, in tune.

The women and girls started screaming
When *ELVIS* walked out on the stage.
The yells got louder and louder,
Coming from people of every age.

A white bell bottom jumpsuit
With rhinestone feathers galore,

And the scarves he placed around his neck,
The crowd kept reaching for.

The songs he sang brought back memories
Of earlier days and nights.
To finally see *ELVIS* in concert,
Was such a welcomed sight!

He belted out, "That's Alright Momma",
"Hound Dog", and "Jailhouse Rock".
And as the hands of time moved on,
We all wanted to stop the clock.

"All Shook Up", "Suspicious Minds",
"Don't Be Cruel", and "Blue Suede Shoes";
"Polk Salad Annie, Gators Got Your Granny",
"Love Me Tender", and "Moody Blue".

He sang the songs most grew up on,
Songs we all knew so well:
"Are You Lonesome Tonight", "Return To Sender",
"Hard Headed Woman", and "Heartbreak Hotel".

"In The Ghetto", "Teddy Bear",
That old one, "It's Now Or Never".
He sang with sass, "A Little Less Conversation",
We could've listened to him forever!

He mixed in some of the newer songs:
Sang "Hurt", "I Got A Woman", "Burning Love";
"Blue Eyes Crying In The Rain",
We knew we'd never hear enough.

As he sang "American Trilogy"
And those velvety high notes he bellowed,

Everyone sat in amazement -
He's such a good lookin' fella!

"I Want You, I Need You, I Love You",
How special he made us all feel!
He sang to us, "I Can't Stop Loving You",
And that moment is in my memory still.

When he, at last closed the concert
With "I Can't Help Falling in Love",
You could've heard a pin drop -
His voice so tender, blessed from above.

We fans still wanted to see more
When He wrapped up the show;
We all wanted a double encore -
None of us was ready to go.

As we filed out of the building
Knowing he had moved our souls,
We all left there in agreement:
He's the "King of Rock and Roll"!

AUTHOR'S NOTE

*On February 21, 1977 my sister-in-law, ***Meta Furr Armstrong** *and I attended Elvis' last concert in Charlotte, North Carolina. Six months later on August 16, 1977, Elvis forever "left the building."*

OF COURSE

It had been awhile since she turned eighteen,
But he still made her feel like a beauty queen.
She noticed those wrinkles, was showing some gray,
But he still loved her like he did in "her day."

He said," I love you girl, nothing's gonna change it,
I love you girl, don't want you to feel no pain, and
I'll protect you with my life, lay it on the line for yours,
Every time you ask if I still love you…I'll say, *Of course!"*

The day they said their wedding vows,
They knew they could make it, but they didn't know how.
Lived in a sad part of town in a rundown shack,
Didn't have much more than the clothes on their backs.

But he'd say, "I love you girl, nothing's gonna change it,
I love you girl, don't want you to feel no pain, and
I'll protect you with my life, lay it on the line for yours,
Every time you ask if I still love you…I'll say, *"Of course!"*

A strong bond they had, it was true love and devotion,
And neither of them, through the years, had ever got the notion,
To slip out on the other, to tear their lives apart,
'Cause ever since they dated, they had locked hearts.

She said, "I love you man, nothing's gonna change it,
I love you man, don't want you to feel no pain, and
I'll protect you with my life, lay it on the line for yours,
Every time you ask if I still love you…I'll say, *Of course!"*

He was in the service. They met at 20 and 23.
Once his lips had touched hers, he knew he had the key,

To her precious heart and he would never betray it,
That's why to this day, you can still hear him say it:

He'll say, "I love you girl, nothing's gonna change it,
I love you girl, don't want you to feel no pain, and
I'll protect you with my life, lay it on the line for yours,
Every time you ask if I still love you…I'll say, *Of course!*"

SCRIPTURE REFERENCES
I Corinthians 13:4-8, 16:14 ~ Colossians 3:14

AUTHOR'S NOTE

Inspired while looking in the mirror at wrinkles gradually forming and thinking of how it feels to have a long-lasting relationship by the grace of God, despite all the struggles of life.

OH DANDELION

Oh dandelion, oh dandelion,
Pretty little plant of spring;
You pop up all over the lawn,
Showing off your golden bling.

During the three phases of your life,
You represent the sun, the moon, and stars;
Most gardeners think you're an aggravation,
But I see how beautiful you are.

The bright yellow petals you display,
Are a reminder of the glorious sun;
The fluffy gray puff ball that follows after,
Represents the moon in its full phases begun.

Your floating seeds give representation
Of the beautiful night time stars;
As they can be carried far, far away
By gusty winds across fields and yards.

As March winds blow and April rains fall,
Your fluffy seed pods drift past my head;
Before I know it, when I look outside,
I'll see not one of you but a million instead.

With a deep breath I blast your parachutes apart,
Catch a flying seed then make a wish;
Even the most unusual places
With your presence have been kissed.

You open up to the world in the morning,
During the day show your full face of delight;
At darkness you close up and go to sleep
When the long day turns to night.

Every part of you is useful,
Master of survival you are;
One can use your roots, leaves, buds, flowers too,
Or just arrange them in a tiny jar.

Useful for food little dandy,
I take my hat off and salute thee;
High in vitamins, good addition to salads,
Boiled, fried... in wine, soups, or tea.

Who knew your uses were so widespread,
Like a first aid kit treating ailments of all kinds;
Toothache, sprain, fever, dandruff -
Your value blows my mind!

Oh dandelion, oh dandelion,
Wafting to your new address unknown;
And when your seed pod gently hits the ground,
Another golden dandelion will be sown.

The children don't get in trouble,
When your pretty stems they break free.
In fact, Mommas say to their children, "How sweet!
Thank you for bringing this flower to me."

AUTHOR'S NOTE

*Dedicated to my youngest son, **Rusty,** who when he was 2 years old, would pick every dandelion bloom he saw to bring to me. I showed excitement over each one and he was so proud. There were so many I started keeping them in a small container–like precious treasures to me still.*

OH LISTEN

Oh listen to the cricket in the black of night,
His chirping you hear, but he's out of sight.

Oh listen to Elvis singing "Blue Suede Shoes",
With his hair slicked back in a perfect swoop.

Oh listen to the rhythm of the windshield wipers,
Raindrops fall but not on the driver.

Oh listen can you hear me calling out to you?
To look at that rainbow of breathtaking hues.

Oh listen to the preacher in the little white church,
Preaching from his heart so all will have heard.

Oh listen to the chestnut Belgian horse neigh,
He's so stout he can pull twenty percent of his weight.

Oh listen to the buzzing of the honeybees,
Search for their sweet honey in the hollow of the tree.

Oh listen to the song as the wind chimes blow,
The wind moves on, going where it wants to go.

Oh listen, it's Bluegrass music with a down home beat,
Sing along, clap your hands, and stomp your feet.

Oh listen to the ducks quack while in the pond,
The ducklings follow Momma as she paddles along.

Oh listen to the owl with his call, "Whooo, Whooo",
If you walk through the woods, he might scare you.

Oh listen to the children in the swing sky high,
They like to go fast and pretend they can fly.

Oh listen to the laughter as old friends commune,
You can tell by their smiles, their hearts are in tune.

Oh listen to the gurgling creek as the waters pass by,
Hope drought doesn't hit and make the creek bed dry.

Oh listen to the snoring right beside me in bed,
If I'm gonna sleep, I've got to cover my head!

SCRIPTURE REFERENCES
Proverbs 20:12, 25:12 ~ Isaiah 30:21 ~ Mark 4:23-24 ~ I Corinthians 2:9

OH LOOK

Oh look at those yellow daffodils,
They look like a blanket covering the hills.

Oh look at that multi-colored balloon of hot air,
Invading blue skies like it just doesn't care.

Oh look at that big bass jump up in the lake,
With shiny scales of silver he then glides away.

Oh look at the orange growing on a Florida tree,
Soon it'll be juice for someone to drink.

Oh look at that shiny gold wedding band,
Expressing the love of a woman and a man.

Oh look at that fire engine painted in red,
Sirens are blazing, let it go ahead!

Oh look at that robin building her nest,
She's recognized by her rust colored breast.

Oh look at that polar bear's fluffy white fur.
He lives in Alaska…"brrrr, brrrr, brrrr"!

Oh look at that fruit bowl filled with green grapes,
I can already tell how good they will taste.

Oh look at that police car's light of bright blue,
Looks like you're in trouble, oh what did you do?

Oh look, it's a flamingo with feathers of pink,
He's quite a long legged fella, dontcha think?

Oh look at that longleaf pine of dark green,
I believe it's the tallest tree I've ever seen!

Oh look at that brown football made of strong leather,
The team's gonna play no matter the weather.

Oh look at that king dressed in his robe of purple,
Show him respect, his dynasty is royal.

Oh look at that stunning cardinal, all dressed in brilliant red,
He's recognized by his feathers, his black mask, and pointy crest.

SCRIPTURE REFERENCES
Proverbs 20:12 ~ Matthew 6:22 ~ I Corinthians 2:9 ~ Ephesians 1:18
Hebrews 12:2

OLD BESSIE

Old Bessie wears a cowbell,
Out in the pasture green.
Her farmer wants to keep up with her,
She's the best Jersey he's ever seen.

Sweet Bessie is a handsome one,
She faithfully gives her milk.
For it a good price the farmer gets,
It tastes good and is smooth as silk.

She walks over to the salt block,
And gives it a few good licks.
Getting many of the nutrients she needs,
Bessie's thirsty, she wants water quick!

Old Bessie meanders down her well worn path,
To drink from her little pond.
Of the geese and the ducks and the frogs down there,
Her bovine heart has grown fond.

In the blazing heat of the summer,
She finds rest under a big old oak.
She dreams of sweet hay and thick green grass,
Glad she's never had to wear a yoke.

As the soft winds blow she lingers,
Giving her cud a few hours of chew.
She's enjoys it so much being lazy,
Old Bessie doesn't even give a "Moo".

ON MY BACK LIKE A TURTLE

Now, I know how a turtle feels
When he gets turned over in his shell.
How you might say can a human know,
What something like that feels, pray tell.

Well, I just had a mastectomy,
The turtle and I have been on the same road.
For the muscles of my chest wall were recently cut,
And the doctor removed lymph nodes.

So the only comfortable way to lie down,
Is to be on my back pretty much.
The only problem with doing that is...
When I get down, it's hard to get up!

Without causing pain, without moving in vain,
As I find myself on my back;
I need help from my husband who's been so sweet,
'Cause to get up on my own, I find lack.

I truthfully need aid from another,
And with hands so kind he lifts up;
Helping me get on my feet again
'Cause like the turtle, it seems I'm stuck.

Yes, I can sympathize with a turtle,
Who finds itself in a mess.
It's funny you see how the turtle and me
Have a lot in common, I guess!

———————⟲∽⟳———————

REMEMBER ALL THIS WHEN I'M OLD

I cook a good meal and have them all over,
I slip them a few extra bucks;
I climb to the attic and find what they need,
I might buy some gas for that truck.

Sometimes I pick up the tab at the restaurant,
On occasion, for mine they will pay;
"Thanks Mom, we really appreciate it,"
That's what they will always say.

I help plan the birthday parties,
Pay for the grandchildren's favorite themed cake;
To show my family just how much I care,
I do whatever it takes.

I tuck goodies into their stockings,
They love pistachios and candy;
If they need any help in decorating,
They call "Mimi" 'cause with that I'm handy.

"Mom, can you do me a favor,
Pick up the kids, since I'm working late?
Can you pick up the oldest from middle school?"
"Sure son, that would be great!"

I go to the mall, to do a little shopping,
Always looking for the latest deal;
Buy something special for the girls,
Share it with them, and love how we all feel.

Borrow this, borrow that,
Whatever's mine is theirs.

Whatever is on their hearts and minds,
Also becomes this Momma's cares.

We get along great, these kids and I,
And when the story is all told,
I laugh and say to my sons and daughters-in-law,
Now, you just *remember all this when I'm old!*

SCRIPTURE REFERENCES
Exodus 20:12 ~ Leviticus 19:3 ~ Deuteronomy 5:16 ~ Ephesians 6:1-4

RETIREMENT

I've worked since 16 for a Social Security Check,
So I was ready when my husband said "RETIRE!"
I hung up my hat, left the hitching post behind,
My work time had forever expired!

All that I could think about was
"NOW I'LL HAVE MORE TIME!"
I never have to go to work again,
" Yippee!" Those words are sublime.

I go to bed real late at night
And get up whenever I want to;
I shop and shop and shop some more
'Til my feet tell my brain we're all through.

I enjoy serving the Lord in many ways,
Taking food to those who are shut in;
And when the notion hits me,
I call on my next of kin.

When the grandkids want to go to the movies
Or play all day in the park,
This "Mimi" is always ready!
We hang out until it's dark.

The vegetables in my garden
Are always in need of tending;
After a while I need to sit down,
As my back hurts from all that bending.

My flowers bloom so beautifully
They take a lot of time;
To me that therapy in the dirt
Is like no other kind.

I pick a bunch of daffodils,
My elderly neighbor enjoys a bouquet;
I sit with her and talk a spell,
I'm told that makes her day.

The cats and dogs, goats and rabbits,
Deserve some loving attention;
But then, my husband also does,
I dare not forget that to mention.

We go about from day to day,
Taking care our business and errands;
Through hospital visits, funerals, texts and calls,
We like to show our caring.

Our time is taken by many things:
Cell phones, social media, the computer;
I even laugh and get on board
When the grandkids bring their scooter.

Cooking, cleaning, playing house
With that sweet man of mine;
We're growing old together
With this *RETIREMENT* life, I'm just fine!

SCRIPTURE REFERENCES
Job 12:12 ~ Psalm 92:12-14 ~ Isaiah 46:4 ~ Titus 2:1-3

———————— ∞ ————————

RUBY THROATED HUMMINGBIRD

Like a mini helicopter
buzzing past my head,
With a tiny throat of scarlet,
Neck feathers glow ruby red.

Your body feathers of metallic green,
Iridescent in the summer sunlight;
Like the intentional dive bomber you are,
A master maneuver of flight.

Amazing little acrobat, you fly backward and upside down.
What a magical creature!
Observing your features
Leaves my head spinning around.

The smallest of their kind
With a high metabolic rate,
Without lots of nectar and our "sugar water",
It's sad, but they will meet their fate.

Speaking of the little bird's size,
An average adult weighs less that a nickel;

Better be careful or predators
Will have him or her in a pickle.

Always keeping a "watchful eye"
Looking out for owls and grackles;
This feisty little creature is not scared,
And those bigger birds it will tackle.

Can really turn a bird watcher's head,
With its elegant blended pattern;
Cream colored ring around its neck,
Reminding us of Saturn.

Around the red glass feeder, hovering in place,
Gives the watcher a "close up" – a good chance to see his face.
With his long, sharp beak and his good eyesight,
He takes off again with all his might.

Rapid wing beats over fifty times per second,
Creating a humming noise;
It's sights like him "birders" love to see,
In the likes they find great joy.

Hummingbirds are very aggressive,
And that aggression is for good reason;
They have to glean their food and mate
While in gleaning and breeding season.

They feel there may not be
Enough food to go around;
So they defend and dart and flit
And chase each other out of town.

Claiming their territory,
While also defending their nest,
It seems other than their mate,

Others are unwelcome guests.

It also truthfully seems,
If not for such good vision,
With another one of its kind,
There would be a bad collision.

Red and orange flowers
Attract their kind so well;
They seek to drink of sweet nectar
Though they have no sense of smell.

Pinto bean sized eggs
In a ping pong ball sized nest;
Woven from spider silk, moss, and leaves,
Once created the female can rest.

The eggs are so, so tiny,
She only lays two at a time;
To let Momma hatch the young and raise,
The Daddy agrees is just fine.

When he drinks from a feeder,
Thirteen times a second he can sip;
When it's finally time to migrate,
He will pack on the weight and get "ripped".

Then hard to believe but typically,
Flying alone up to 500 miles per day;
Keeping the pedal to the metal,
With not much time to stop along the way.

When you realize you're not seeing them anymore,
You'll know they're headed to another nation;
Well goodbye sweet hummingbird, see ya next year,
When you repeat your spring migration.

SANDWICH GENERATION

Those my age are called "Baby Boomers",
We've also been called the *"Sandwich Generation"*;
Because at our prime, we were sandwiched in,
Between our parents, and the children of our procreation.

We had parents who were elderly
While we were at the age of life;
When it was their turn, to need help from us,
And we could've turned them down, but why?

Besides parents, we also had children,
Some still at home, some left the nest;
There was education to pay for, ends to make meet,
Not to mention, all the stress of the rest!

Time went by so fast,
We had demanding jobs to be at;
Hurry, hurry, rush, rush, rush,
There were headaches, and deadlines to be met.

Health problems, world issues and the like,
Would we have a job tomorrow?
Would the company go on strike,
Would we live with hearts in sorrow?

Not too many times,
Could we feel completely carefree;
There was so much to worry about:
Rarely ever felt at ease

Always planning for the future
With an IRA, Savings or 401K;

Looking out for everyone,
And especially for our own golden days.

We made it through all that just fine,
But now, some of us need aid too;
Up to this point, we've done our best,
Taking care of parents and our children as they grew.

Things have changed, we're on down the road,
Many of us have been able to retire;
It's slowed down a tad for quite a few,
With our feet not held as closely to the fire.

But now, some have children up for non support
As times are hard, the world grows colder;
We're raising grandchildren of their divorce,
Raising children is not as easy when you're older.

Oh don't think that we're complaining,
We're not even making a fuss;
But kids, as we gradually get older,
We pray you'll take good care of us!

STUFF

Do you like *stuff* like I do?
It's gathered all around -
On shelves, in boxes, on dressers.
I really do like *stuff*, I've found.

Yard sales, gifts, collections -
My house is full it's true;
When I look at some of my *stuff*
It reminds me of friends like you.

Birthdays, Christmases, sickness -
All these have been occasions,
When you have given *stuff* to me
To give my spirit a raising.

I love my *stuff*, yes, it's the truth,
It brings much joy to me;
My attic is so full it bulges,
But I think more *stuff* I need.

I know I can't take it with me,
I'll leave it all behind one day;
But while I live and yet still breathe,
Please don't take any of my *stuff* away!

STUFFED ANIMALS

They need one of them to go to sleep,
As to the Lord they pray, their souls to keep.
Find a favorite *stuffed animal*,
Get "Mack" or "The Big Red Dog".
It really doesn't matter,
As sleep comes over like a fog.

"I want this one!" "No, you take that one!"
I sense a problem as they begin to chatter.

Hey, hey it's not important, just decide!
Well I guess, maybe it does really matter.

Get to sleep or I'll take them all away,
In grandmotherly love I chide;
Now be kind to one another,
Don't let a *stuffed animal* your love divide.

Well good, it's over, they're asleep now,
But I hear as the new day breaks -
A little whining, a little whimper,
What of that sound do I make?

Someone needs to have that comfort,
Someone needs to feel that touch,
Of that beloved sometimes well worn *stuffed animal,*
That little children grow to love so much.

THAT OLD HANDKERCHIEF

I have a soiled, *old handkerchief*
I've kept it through the years.
You might wonder why, to it I've held on,
'Cause, it's stained, from make-up and tears.

I cried till my soul was weary;
I cried till I felt so weak;
I cried my groanings into that *old handkerchief,*
When no words, I could find to speak.

My heart called out for mercy;
"Oh God, send me relief.
This pain I'm feeling, I've never felt before;
Never, ever known this much grief."

He touched my broken heart that night,
Whispered to my soul, "Be still."
He cradled me, it truly felt,
As my wounded spirit, He began to heal.

So, I'm looking at that dirty, *old handkerchief,*
With black marks from tear filled eyes;
As I remember those stormy days gone by,
I'm gratefully thanking Him now, for blue skies.

AUTHOR'S NOTE

*Psalms 18:6 In my distress, **I CALLED UPON THE LORD**, and **CRIED** unto my God: **HE HEARD** my voice out of His temple, and my cry came before Him, even into His ears*

THE BROKEN ANGEL

Grandma baked Christmas cookies
Shaped as angels, trees, bells, and stars.
Lovingly she formed them and placed them in her cookie jar.
When the grandkids would come over, they would always run to see
If grandma had baked some cookies... and there they would always be.
Grandma loved her babies and took such great delight
In seeing their little eyes light up, at such delicious sights.

Angels, trees, bells, and stars disappeared before she knew it.
She loved to bake, her cookies were great, and love was what caused her to do it.
The kids all came over one evening and straight to her jar they ran.
"Come give me a hug before cookies you get!
Do you love cookies more than your gran?"
Hugs and kisses they all gave her, and when she'd had her fill,
They were allowed to pick out their favorites, as on the table they spilled.

One day grandma was hungry and headed for the cookie jar.
Only one little cookie was left behind, because it had fallen apart.
She picked up all the pieces and as on the table they laid,
She put them together like a puzzle and the shape of an angel they made.
As dimming eyes and feeble hands placed piece beside of piece,
God spoke to her heart reminding her of His amazing grace.....

Of the many days in her *journey,* the brokenness of life she'd felt.
Then there at her kitchen table, the old grandmother knelt.
"Thank you God for healing deep hurts along the way.
For strength and health and happiness you've brought from day to day.
The *journey* has not been easy. Satan's vice has gripped my heart.
I knew from the day I made you my Lord, he would send out his fiery darts.

But you, oh Lord have been faithful, a compassionate friend I see.
Your mercies are new every morning and your love grows more precious to me.
When troubles and trials would break me, destroying my will to live,
You've mended your *broken angel* with the love only you could give."

SCRIPTURE REFERENCES
Psalm 147:3 ~ Lamentations 3:22-23 ~ Ephesians 6:16

THE COLOR PINK

I've always liked the *color pink,*
But pink has taken on new meaning.
Because of events in my life
And this year's mammogram screening.

Hearing the words, BREAST CANCER,
Was really pretty tough.
Radiation, chemo, mastectomy -
Hearing all that was too much!

I know I'm not the only one,
I'm certainly not the Lone Ranger;
Many women before me and after,
Breast cancer has and will put in danger.

Now when any article of pink I see
I'm always reminded of,
The fact that it represents an awareness
Of breast cancer and of others' love.

God designed women so uniquely,
Strong willed and power housed;
Yet tender and compassionate,
With mercy and kindness doused.

Nowadays there's something special
About that beautiful *color of pink;*
When I see it, I'm touched so deeply,
As of my dear breast cancer "sisters" I think.

*Dedicated to all of my **breast cancer "sisters"**, especially the memory of my long time family friend, **Mary Alice Ballard Love**. I'll never forget the day the Lord nudged me to visit her. I found her in tears. She led me to the bathroom where in the sink, much of her hair had fallen. I held her and our tears mixed. We both knew that God had ordained my visit and before my departure, we ended up laughing as we reminisced, shared experiences, and pondered the goodness of God even through our breast cancer journeys.*

THE DIFFERENCE YOU'LL SEE IN ME

I'm just an old chunk of coal right now,
But I'm gonna be a diamond one day.
I'll take my flight and clear this Earth
When God calls me away.

I'm slowly in the process
Of becoming what God wants me to be;
What you see before you now
Is not all HE has for me.

This world and all its pressures,
This life and all its stress,
Will gladly be left behind one day
When God calls me to rest.

The difference in a flawless diamond
And a dirty black piece of coal,
Will be *the difference you'll see in me*
When I'm walking on streets of gold!

*Written in honor of my "Daddy", **Ralph C. Flowe** just days after he took his flight to Heaven.*

THE LIZARD

One day as I walked in my bedroom,
There on the carpet it laid,
What I thought at first was an oak leaf,
Was a creature of whose kind I'm afraid!
A *lizard* I saw with my own eyes.
So still and silent was he.
Oh my! What a shocker! Do something!
Is this a real *lizard* I see?
I thought of how I might get him.
And just how did he get in here?
Oh my! What am I going to do?
Dear Lord, you know my fear!
Let me think. Oh, I've just bought groceries.
Yes, I've been to the grocery store.
That's it! He made himself welcome
As I carried all those bags through the door.
As I pondered my course of destruction,
A thought entered into my mind.
Grab the newspaper! Just throw it at him!
Hurry up, you don't have much time!
Oh no! I missed him, he's vanished!
Underneath the dresser he went.
I won't give up that easily.

In more foolish ways, time I've spent.
Come out from there, you coward.
I'll not leave my post.
If you're not outta here by bedtime,
Of being up all night, I'll boast.
I'll never sleep a wink,
My husband knows that's true.
But he's not here to help me...
So it's just me against you.
Having visions of you on my bedspread
Or crawling across my pillow -
I'm getting weak. I'm feeling faint.
Much like a sappy willow.
Get hold of yourself. It's just a lizard.
Who's the smarter of you two?
Well, I don't know, but there he is again....
Now what am I going to do?
I thought to myself, "Throw the paper,
And get rid of him for good."
Well, it worked, and now he's a goner.
His body lies deep in the woods!

———————— ∽ ————————

THE OLD POTTING SHED

Garden soil, clay pots, and snippers
Potting soil and spades and clippers

Scissors and Dad's old rusty hammer
Ornamental flags and seasonal banners

Aprons and a red yard wagon
Rope and twine to keep vines from sagging

Little glass jars to root tender cuttings
Mosquito spray to avoid itchy rubbing

A gazing ball and a cat bed too
Trellises and a ladder just to name a few

Bug spray, black spot, and snail prevention
Sometimes some plants need special attention

Last spring's seeds in a plastic bag
Souvenirs from fun trips I've had

A couple worn out gardening books
Lots and lots of shelves and hooks

Hanging baskets that'll soon be full
Spanish Moss and yard art so cool

Little gnomes, squirrels, and the like
Hanging up high is my childhood bike

Butterflies and bees on metal stakes
Shovels, hoes, augers, and rakes

Plastic pots of every hue
Feeders for my hummingbird juice

Birdhouses, a birdbath, and suet fruity
Bulbs of all kinds that will produce great beauty

Pictures of roosters and wordy signs
A clock on the wall to give the time

Shepherd hooks, bags of fertilizer
Don't be alarmed, don't let nothing surprise ya

About a dozen well used tiki torches
Lanterns and lights for my sidewalk and porches

An old tired broom with bristles missin'
Two porcelain love birds on their nest a kissin'

A Merry Tiller with good sharp tines
Sets of bamboo and colored glass wind chimes

Sun catchers stuck on window panes
Multiple cans of pretty wood stains

All colors of spray paint to freshen dull things
Even a bowl full of flower pot bling

Gloves to save my nails and hands
A container of well used sandbox sand

A box of all sized nails just in case
An umbrella to keep the rain off my face

A thing-a-ma-jig for reaching up high
When tiptoes don't work, on it I rely

It looks like I'm running out of space
But made room for one more sign says..."SAVED BY GRACE"

A kneeling bench, muddy garden shoes
Yes, it sounds like a lot but all this stuff I use

The older I am, the more tired I get
But I'll never get tired of THE OLD POTTING SHED.

SCRIPTURE REFERENCES
Ecclesiastes 3:12-13

THE PARK

Hey, wanna go to the *park* today?
To let down your hair, to romp and play?
Your imagination is sure to run wild,
Go ahead and bring out that inner child.
Where are the swings? Oh, goodness what fun!
Playing in the park, taking in the sun.
Slipping and sliding, hanging from monkey bars,
Hide and seek, watch out for the cars!
Picnics and laughter, observing God's creation,
There's no better day than one used for recreation.

SCRIPTURE REFERENCES
Ecclesiastes 8:15 ~ Zechariah 8:5 ~ Mark 6:31

THE PARKING LOT WALL

One morning as I was facing
Trouble like I had never seen,
I sat in my car praying
Before work as my custom had been.

My heart was burdened and so heavy,
I didn't know what to do.
Seeking the Lord for wisdom,
I said, "Lord you know I trust you."

The words came quickly out of my mouth;
My heart was overflowing.
What will tomorrow send my way?

Where is my future going?

My vehicle was parked so closely
To a wall, it was all I could see.
As I heard the Lord speak to my spirit,
"Child, you can depend on me.

In the natural, all that's before you,
Is a wall of doubt and fear.
But look up higher than the concrete,
For you there's a message clear."

I leaned up toward the steering wheel,
To the top of the wall I could see....
Weeds, grass, briars, and dead clutter.
What could His message be?

Then a vine of sweet honeysuckle
Suddenly caught my eye.
"OK, Lord, I get it....
You're telling me on you to rely.

Right now all things look gloomy;
Right now my way is sad;
You're telling me to keep looking up;
One day you'll make me glad!

Lord, you're like that perfumy honeysuckle,
Your love and precious Word guide;
In the bitterness of life's winters,
To my life, sweet fragrance you provide."

The sweetness of that moment
Only my broken spirit knows;
When I'm faced again with new troubles,
To the wall in that parking lot I go.

SCRIPTURE REFERENCES

Psalm 92:12-14 ~ Jeremiah 29:13 ~ II Corinthians 2:15 ~ Hebrews 12:2

————— ∽ —————

THE PLANT LADY

It was early spring and the grass began growing,
By the calendar I knew it was time;
To get on down to the plant farm,
And become a gardener part time.

It's in my blood to be a gardener,
Mom and both grandmothers had plants of all sorts;
I guess I got the "bug" from them,
They each grew beautiful flowers, in short.

My husband and I drove down there,
His goal was veggie plants and seeds;
We took the truck cause it's got a nice bed,
He never knows what he's bringing home with me!

Got there, went straight to the hanging baskets,
Picked out my Boston and Asparagus Ferns;
Mulled over the others choosing the best,
My loving husband sat waiting unconcerned.

Bent down, looking over the begonias,
A tall lady with a hat came my way;
I looked up at her and her face just glowed,
I said, "How are you doing today?"

In her arms she cradled pink petunias,
Pretty gray hair spilled from her wide brim hat;

Her plan was to plant them in a window box,
She shared as we began to chat.

We struck up a friendly conversation,
Felt like I'd known that woman for years;
We talked about all kinds of things,
Some things she said brought a tear.

The more we shared about flowers and such,
I saw she was a beautiful soul;
Told me she'd "done taxes" till the age of eighty,
Her late husband was on the State Highway Patrol.

Her years of work were one way she showed love,
Seemed she had a full, active life;
Told me she had a son and grandchildren,
Loved her roles of mom, grandmother, and wife.

I told her about my family
As we talked about our kin;
She lives in nearby Mt. Pleasant,
Knew my "Granny Flowe" and many more of them.

There was a common bond
As we spoke across the aisle;
We covered many subjects,
And she had the sweetest smile.

Her eyes beamed and her heart was warm,
She was a believer, too, I could see;
Thought to myself, "If I live to ninety one,
She's exactly how I want to be."

We'd both like to join a garden club,
'Cause we enjoy discussing plants and flowers;

She spoke with so much wisdom and grace,
I could have talked to her for hours.

It was so refreshing as we communicated
About everything from A-Z;
There in the middle of the greenhouse
While my man still waited patiently.

The idea came to me suddenly,
So I mentioned my poetry book;
Told her I'd love to write a poem about her
And take her picture, 'cause I loved her cute look!

She headed to the counter to pay for her plants,
As our conversation would end;
Saw my husband and said, "Nice to meet you.
Met your wife, now I've got a new friend."

We only shared a brief moment in time,
But by her I was truly impressed;
It was great to run into another like me,
Who with the love of gardening is possessed.

If you live in the town of Mt Pleasant,
Chances are, you just might know her;
The precious *plant lady* I encountered that day
By the name of Mrs. Bernice Cloninger.

———————— ∽ ————————

THE RABBIT RIDE

If you see a camouflaged monster
Coming down the road toward you,
Don't be alarmed, it's only a Suburban
Painted with its colors all subdued.

It was bought back in the 90's
When my husband came to say,
"I found a good deal on a truck to fix up,
So the guys can ride together on hunting days."

Next, the paint and the patterns were purchased,
Army green, black, tan, and brown.
They worked for a day, my husband and sons,
And you can't miss it if it comes to your town!

They lovingly named it "*The Rabbit Ride*",
And each Saturday when season is in,
You'll find my family up early,
Getting well trained dogs from their pens.

They stop somewhere for breakfast,
Then to that old truck and back in.
I love them so much they are precious to me,
My three very favorite men.

After the hunt is over,
The guns safely in the truck rack,
They open the cooler and pull out
A big plastic bag full of snacks.

Viennas, crackers, Little Debbies,
Sundrop, Cheerwine, and Coke,

From purchasing dog food, gas, shells, and snacks,
It's a wonder my husband ain't broke!

They stand around retracing,
The hunt and the steps of the day.
Then after much laughter and practical jokes,
My hunters are back on their way.

It's toward home they're all now headed.
What a good day it has been!
Just look if you think you can find them,
'Cause it's a camouflaged *rabbit ride* they're in.

Like a page from a "find-it" book, hunt them,
They and their camouflaged friends.
Look good! It'll be hard to spot them.
Yes, all you will see is big grins!

AUTHOR'S NOTE

*My husband and sons (**Mitchell, Keith and Rusty**) love to hunt. Through the years, they have enjoyed a lot of fellowship with each other and good friends in that old, camouflaged truck.*

THE REDBUDS

The Redbuds bloom on Hwy 49
Suggesting to all passersby
The world is in a transition stage
And that spring has just arrived.

They're everywhere along the banks
Between the oaks, the elms and pine trees.
They say nothing at all as I drive by,
But their beauty speaks loudly to me.

THE TOUCH LAMP

There is an old *touch lamp* on the nightstand,
That sits on his side of the bed;
I removed it from there for a little while,
With plans to put a more stylish one there instead.

But when he came to bed and saw it was gone,
"Where's my *touch lamp?*" he excitedly said.
I told him my plans then with a grim protest,
He shared what was in his head.

"Who cares if it looks best or not?
It's convenient when I hop into bed.
I only have to reach and barely touch that lamp.
Don't use another one there." he said.

That change was just a minor thing,
But to him it was a big deal.
So I showed some respect and thought about
How my choice had made him feel.

I acquiesced, retrieved that old lamp,
And put it back on his table;
Now to sleep at night in unity,
It's for sure that I am able.

At night when we get into bed
With that old lamp in his view,
He smiles, kisses me, and turns off the *touch lamp*
Saying, "Honey, do you know how much I love you?"

SCRIPTURE REFERENCES
Psalm 133:1 ~ Romans 14:19 ~ II Corinthians 13:11 ~ Ephesians 4:2-3
I Peter 3:8

There's a Song Stuck In My Head

I hear a song on the radio
Or somebody starts up singing;
Throughout the day within my head
That tune constantly keeps ringing.

Its lyrics haunt me at each turn
Trying to get it off my brain;
But from rehearsing over and over its words
Can't make myself refrain.

Each phrase and syllable has got me stuck,
Feels like I'm under a spell;
Feels like I've done something wrong,
Been put in "earworm" jail.

Drum beats repeat in my subconscious,
It's true, I really love this song;
Even though the singer has great pipes,
I hate how it won't leave me alone!

Can't keep this up, gotta move on,
Gonna drive me batty, I know;
'Cause when I put my mind in drive,
It doesn't want to go.

It's getting late, I'm tired and sleepy,
There's a song stuck in my head;
I just don't know what else to do,
I've even brought that song to bed!

THERE'S A WELL

There's a well in a foreign country
Dug and paid for by a ministry I support.
Those living there walked miles to draw water
With barrels, buckets, jugs, and the sort.

My heart was filled with compassion
Seeing pictures of filthy, muddy water.
Knowing all I need do is turn on a faucet
When their water caused need for a doctor.

I heard a missionary say one time
When asked what she missed about "The States":
Her answer was "taking a nice, hot shower"
She had given up that pleasure for Christ's sake.

I saw pictures of children with dirty feet
As they drank from a cup of orange liquid.
I heard many were dying, distressed, and diseased
As their young bodies with parasites were inflicted.

The cattle had stepped into the water source,
Upstream taking care of their business.
When all these things I began to consider,
I thought I must give, I cannot do less!

I trust this ministry, they truly love God,
So to give for a well, my heart agreed.
Then in the mail with a "thank-you" note,
Pictures of their clean water later came to me.

As the metal auger and casing
Bore down deep into the ground,
Aqua was brought forth gushing sky high,
A new water source was found!

The children had smiles as they played in the mist,
And the sight brought tears to my eyes.
To them it was like a fun playground,
Like a well planned out surprise.

They drank safe water, that before was unknown,
And they frolicked and played with great joy.
It made me so thankful for the clean water here
And reminded me of my own little boys.

I never had to cook their food
Feeling like I was leading them to the slaughter.
Or made their clothes to look even dirtier,
Never bathed them in a tub of nasty water.

It's something we take for granted,
The wells that have been dug for today.
The lakes, the streams, the rivers, the sources...
Of clean water where we live and play.

SCRIPTURE REFERENCES
Isaiah 12:3, 44:3, 49:10 ~ Matthew 10:42

AUTHOR'S NOTE

*Dedicated to **Marsha Harker Wilson**, the missionary quoted in this poem. Marsha, and her family have served for over 16 years and are currently located in Pacaja, Brazil.*

THRILL SEEKER

Would you ride a roller coaster
With your arms high in the air?
Would you jump off a river bridge
Without giving it a care?

Would you climb inside a pit full of snakes?
Oh goodness, that's not me!
I call myself a *thrill seeker* too,
But around snakes I cannot be.

Would you walk a long, skinny tight rope,
Clutching it with your toes?
Would you not be worried one little bit
Of how much farther you had to go?

Would you climb out on a rickety limb
Of a fragile, old oak tree?
While friends call you a "ding-a-ling",
You say, "Hey ya'll, look at me!"

Do you take others up on their deal,
When a friendly bet they place?
Just to see how long you can hold out,
With a flame held up to your face.

At Halloween during trick-or-treat,
Would you go on a haunted trail?
When the chainsaws come out would you stay put,
While the others around you bail?

Would you stand on the seat of a motorcycle
While racing down the road?
You get all the attention on the street,
While your balancing skills you show.

Would you step out of a high-flying plane,
From way up in the atmosphere?
Would you say to everyone up there,
"Oh, I love it way up here!"

Daredevil you are, doing dangerous things,
Not giving consideration of possible pain.
Risks that bother others, don't bother you at all,
They don't even put your nerves in a strain.

Would you place an apple on top of your head,
To be hit with a bow and arrow?
(When the shooter hasn't shot in years,
And you know your chances are narrow.)

Do you like true excitement,
Crazy and so very intense?
(That you would you lock horns with a raging bull,
In the middle of an arena fence.)

Are you the kind who'll take some risk?
Are you an adrenaline junkie?
Do you not mind putting yourself
In situations that can get unlucky ?

Do you pursue experiences
That bring those thrilling sensations?
If you keep doing this kind of stuff,
You might become a hospital patient.

If any of these you'd care to do
And do them each with pride,
Considering yourself scared of nothing -
As a *thrill seeker* you could be classified!

TRUE LOVE

Some have never known,
True love I've often thought;
Throughout their entire lifetime,
It's *true love* that some have sought.

Well let me tell you brother,
Let me tell you sis,
The truest, most unconditional love
Is not found in a Mr. or a Miss.

Sure, we connect with our special person,
Sometimes it's till death do us part;
Sometimes it's till one rejects the other,
Due to a difference of heart.

So, human love is faulty,
Of that fact there is no doubt;
But the truest love that was ever shown,
Jesus' death taught us all about.

SCRIPTURE REFERENCES
John 3:16, 15:13 ~ Romans 8:38-39

WATER TRAIL

So gracefully the clear water in the creek
Moves slowly around the bend;
It meanders down from the hilltops,
Where does it ever end?

It runs into the gurgling stream,
And its waters begin to have force;
Listen to it speaking....
One can almost hear its voice.

Keeps swelling across the canyon,
Across the meadow wide;
It is a mighty river now,
Making its way down to the tide.

Widest of our land water resources,
Into the lake, some mighty rivers run;
With great beauty for fishing and recreation,
"Go jump in a lake!" we say for fun.

Some rivers find their way through the valleys,
Where to the lowest elevation they go;

Our life-giving water ends up in the ocean,
Into the deep sea, the *water trail* flows.

WEAR OUT, DON'T RUST OUT

Wear out, don't rust out!
An old-time preacher said.
That was his heart's desire,
And he lived that way till death.

Such a precious servant of God
Always visiting, shepherding, and preaching.
He went to many places
On his mission, lost souls to be reaching.

He faithfully and fervently spoke one night
For a "revival" at the church my family attended.
And when he poured his heart out in words,
I knew on Jesus my soul depended.

Because of his profound, yet simple sermon
Plain enough for a child to understand,
I decided to follow Jesus,
Now, I'm bound for the Promised Land!

He served in love and humility
Till he could go no longer;
Because of his caring and convicting preaching,
My faith became much stronger.

He presented his body as the Apostle Paul urged,
Nothing short of a living sacrifice;
His life inspired many others,
Such a willing servant of Christ.

Wear out, don't rust out!
That faithful man of God always said.
He loved the Lord, and he loved people,
And he carried that motto till death.

SCRIPTURE REFERENCES
Matthew 28:19 ~ Romans 10:17, 12:1-2 ~ I Timothy 2:7 ~ II Timothy 2:15
Titus 3:8

AUTHOR'S NOTE

*Dedicated to the memory of **Rev. Victor Lee Trivette**, who was faithful to his call to preach God's Word and thereby my eternal destiny was changed.*

WHAT IF

What would happen if you couldn't?
Then probably someone else could.
What would happen if you didn't?
Then probably someone else would.
What would happen if you shouldn't?
Then probably someone else should.
What if those probabilities all worked out?...
Then probably it would be good!

WHERE ARE MY GLASSES

Where are my glasses?
I can't see a lick!
I can hear the clock ticking,
But I can't see it tick.

Maybe I left them on the counter,
Let me look inside my purse.
Oh goodness, I can't see anything,
And nothing could be worse.

I know they're around here somewhere,
'Cause I just had them on.
Good grief, where did I lay them?
I'm embarrassed to say they're gone.

Think I'll go look in the closet,
Maybe they're up on the rack.
Let me now check in the cabinet
From where I just grabbed a snack.

When I take them off,
I always put them in the same place.
Well, I haven't done that lately
'Cause they get lost when they leave my face!

In the morning when I'm looking,
Find them on the table beside my bed.
In the evening when I'm searching,
I feel and they're on top of my head.

At times, the search leads to frustration;
I say, "Lord please help me find them!"

"You're going to wear Him out with that prayer,"
My husband jokingly says on a whim.

"Oh no, the Lord knows my need,
So that's never the case you see;
He knows exactly where they are,
And I'm just asking Him to show me!"

———————— ∽ ————————

WIND CHIME

God, I hear you speaking to me
From outside on the back porch;
Your voice is in the form of a *wind chime*....
It lights my soul like a torch.

Ting, ting, ting, the metal clicks
As my hummingbird chime make its noise;
To believe it's you, the one true God,
Causing that beautiful sound is my choice.

"I love you," the clangs say to my heart
As the bluster continues to swell;
It's not just pretty noise that I'm hearing,
And that, my soul knows right well.

It's you, gently reminding me
That the wind is in your control;
And from its force, you make beautiful sounds
As you speak your love to my soul.

———————— ∽ ————————

CPSIA information can be obtained
at www.ICGtesting.com
Printed in the USA
BVHW080304031121
620550BV00016B/817